MODERN WORLD NATIONS

MODERN WORLD NATIONS

Taiwan

Christopher L. Salter

Series Consulting Editor
Charles F. Gritzner
South Dakota State University

CHELSEA HOUSE
PUBLISHERS
A Haights Cross Communications Company

Philadelphia

Dedication
To Allen and Jean Lovejoy, and J.R. Wu

Frontispiece: Flag of Taiwan

Cover: The Chiang Kai-shek Memorial Hall was built to commemorate the life of the leader of Nationalist China who moved his government, the Republic of China, into exile on Taiwan after his defeat at the hands of Mao Tse-tung in 1949.

CHELSEA HOUSE PUBLISHERS

VP, NEW PRODUCT DEVELOPMENT Sally Cheney
DIRECTOR OF PRODUCTION Kim Shinners
CREATIVE MANAGER Takeshi Takahashi
MANUFACTURING MANAGER Diann Grasse

Staff for TAIWAN

EXECUTIVE EDITOR Lee Marcott
PRODUCTION EDITOR Megan Emery
ASSISTANT PHOTO EDITOR Noelle Nardone
SERIES DESIGNER Takeshi Takahashi
COVER DESIGNER Keith Trego
LAYOUT 21st Century Publishing and Communications, Inc.

A Haights Cross Communications ✦ Company

http://www.chelseahouse.com

First Printing

1 3 5 7 9 8 6 4 2

Library of Congress Cataloging-in-Publication Data

Salter, Christopher L.
  Taiwan / by Christopher Salter.
    v. cm. — (Modern world nations)
  Contents: Natural landscapes — The historical geography of Taiwan — People and culture — The political geography of Taiwan — Economy — Regional identities — Taiwan in the future.
  ISBN 0-7910-7914-7
  1. Taiwan—Juvenile literature. [1. Taiwan.] I. Title. II. Series.
  DS799.S26 2004
  951.24'9—dc22

2003027777

Table of Contents

Taiwan

CHAPTER

1

Taiwan: A Parallel Universe?

Taiwan, an island lying less than 100 miles (165 kilometers) off the east coast of the People's Republic of China, is first noted in Western records has having been "discovered" by the Portuguese in 1590. They named the tobacco-leaf-shaped island "Ilha Formosa," or "Beautiful Island." The name that is more common today is Taiwan, thought to mean "terraced bay," for the active terrace building that has taken place during the past three centuries on the western flanks of the mountains that slope westward toward the Taiwan Strait.

Before the Portuguese found it (and later tried to settle it), the Chinese had known this place as "Bao Dao" or, as geographer Barbara Weightman observes:

[The Chinese] referred to it as "a mudball across the sea, not worthy of China." Bao Dao was known to Chinese fishermen and pirates but was inhabited by non-Chinese people . . .

8

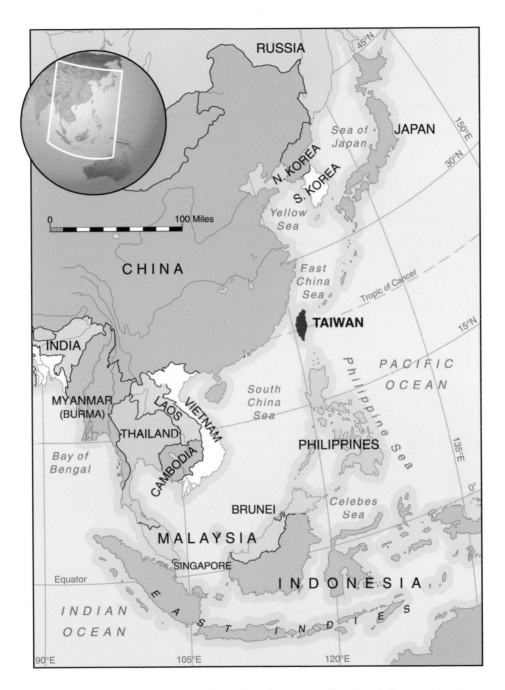

Taiwan is a small country lying less than 100 miles (165 kilometers) off the coast of China. This map shows Taiwan's location and size in relation to its surrounding countries.

[who were] Malay-Polynesian and are related to the indigenous people of the mountains of northern Luzon, the closest island of the Philippines.

The island is approximately twice the size of New Jersey or half again as large as Maryland. Its 13,969-square-mile (35,980-square-kilometer) area is home to more than 22,457,000 people. Lying off the eastern edge of one of the largest countries in the world, Taiwan has an area of just barely one-third of 1 percent the area of the massive China mainland lying just 90 miles (145 kilometers) west. Its population does not quite amount to one-fifth of 1 percent of the mainland country's population, which is the world's largest.

Yet when you read or hear of East Asia and the economics and politics of that major world region, you get images of Taiwan as a major player of the past, present, and certainly the future—a fact that helps us all to realize that it is not necessarily geographical size that defines the importance of any political place or world landscape. Dimensions of importance relate to a whole world of factors. Your study of Taiwan in this book will help you learn what geographical and historical elements create the real significance of places and populations.

Free your mind from the present so that you can see this island lying near traditional mid-seventeenth-century fishing routes along the south-central coast of China. For much of that century, there was discord in China as a Chinese dynasty—the Ming—was being replaced by the non-Chinese Manchu dynasty. From the early 1700s, people were leaving the coastal provinces of China in the pursuit of freedom from this political chaos. Taiwan served as a reasonably close destination for people in flight. By crossing the Taiwan Strait (about the same width as the strait between the island of Cuba and Florida), these migrants were able to get to a place where Chinese was already spoken in many locales. Although the island was less advanced than the mainland, it was more stable than the China they were leaving.

Two centuries later—in the middle of the nineteenth

century—there was another period of difficulty in mainland China (the Taiping Rebellion), and some Chinese people again looked eastward for a safe haven. Taiwan fulfilled that role, although not in as complete a way as it had at the end of the Ming dynasty. Then, in the 1940s and 1950s, this process was realized one more time. This last migration was the biggest the island of Taiwan had ever experienced: some 1,800,000 to 2,000,000 Chinese Nationalists fled mainland China seeking a haven on Taiwan.

In 1895, Taiwan had been ceded to Japan as part of the Treaty of Shimonoseki that concluded the Sino-Japanese War of 1894–1895. From that time until October 1945, Taiwan had been a Japanese colony. From late 1944 through 1945—as the tide of World War II was turning increasingly against the Japanese—they began to make more concessions to the Chinese on the island. With the defeat of the Japanese in the summer of 1945, the six million Chinese living on Taiwan eagerly anticipated independence with the departure of the Japanese in the fall of 1945. Instead, as noted in Rubenstein's *Taiwan: A New History*:

> The inhabitants [of Taiwan] were not even given a chance to indicate their preferences for citizenship, as had been done in 1895, despite the fact that most had loyally supported Japan's wartime effort and had suffered wartime deprivations and casualties, although to a lesser extent than in 1895. As a consequence, the Taiwanese once more came to be governed by "outsiders"—only this time they would be dominated by the Kuomintang [Chinese Nationalists] and mainlander Chinese instead of by Japanese colonial authorities. . . .

In 1949, a civil war that had been raging in various regions of China for more than 20 years came to a conclusion. The Chinese Nationalists (Kuomintang, or KMT)—led by Generalissimo Chiang Kai-shek and supported by the United States—were losing their last bases of support to their opposition, the

Chinese Communists. From as early as 1947 and all through 1949, and especially after the October 1, 1949 declaration of victory by the Communists and Chairman Mao Tse-tung, this migration had been growing in size. Military men and their families—and great quantities of art and portable personal wealth—were moved across the Taiwan Strait as new households were established on the island. A similar unwanted importation of a governing and upper class had taken place just half a century earlier.

With the political change and ongoing migration, Taiwan's Chinese population went from some six million to nearly eight million.

The current drama of Taiwan—at the outset of the twenty-first century—has taken its form from the arrival, growth, development, and ambition of this most recent major Chinese migration. Under the Japanese, the transportation networks, industrial base, and agricultural productivity of Taiwan had been more actively developed than ever before. The Japanese government had envisioned Taiwan as a key location in its anticipated Greater East Asia Co-Prosperity Sphere—a group of countries, including China and the countries of Southeast Asia, that Japan anticipated gaining through its early string of military victories in the early years of World War II. Good harbors on the west and north sides of the island and the island's increasingly productive agriculture led the Japanese to decide to invest considerable capital and manpower in this colonial experiment.

That plan came to an abrupt end in 1945 with Japan's unconditional surrender to the United States and the end of the war. By the 1960s, the KMT had begun to fully understand the economic and political potential this island represented. With that understanding came expansive economic development. This growth helps to explain how this small place has gained such a big role in today's East Asian world.

As you study the island of Taiwan, you will learn about the economic, demographic (population), and political changes that

As it enters the twenty-first century, Taiwan is a distinctive island nation with an expansive economy, diverse population and fascinating landscape. Mount Chu, seen in this photograph, is one of Taiwan's many breathtaking natural landmarks.

have been a part of its historical and contemporary geography. You will also see how political decisions made half a world away have had an enormous impact on the island country and have provided a stimulus for the continual anxiety surrounding its existence. It is this mix of local and distant, economic and political, Chinese and non-Chinese influences that gives Taiwan its truly distinctive importance at the beginning of the twenty-first century.

As you read these pages, think about other relatively small islands located adjacent to large countries and whose history has exerted an unusual influence on events occurring in the much larger mainland. Taiwan is somewhat like a parallel universe to the People's Republic of China; look for further parallels as you learn more of this fascinating landscape and its often-turbulent human history.

2

Natural Landscapes

AREA AND LANDFORMS

Taiwan is a classic example of the geographic phenomenon in which the peak of a submarine mountain range reaches through and above the ocean's surface to form an island. To the east of the island, there are major ocean depths of more than 20,000 feet (6,100 meters). To the west lies the relatively shallow Taiwan Strait (also known as the Formosa Strait). The strait reaches a depth of no more than 500 feet (150 meters). Rivers pour down from the crest of Taiwan's Chung Yang Shan massif (Central Mountain Range) that is 10–35 miles (16–56 kilometers) wide and runs from near the southern tip of the island all the way to the Taipei Basin in the north. The island stretches approximately 235 miles (378 kilometers) from north to south and, on average, 90 miles (145 kilometers) from east to west. Taiwan's coastline measures about 550 miles (890 kilometers) in length.

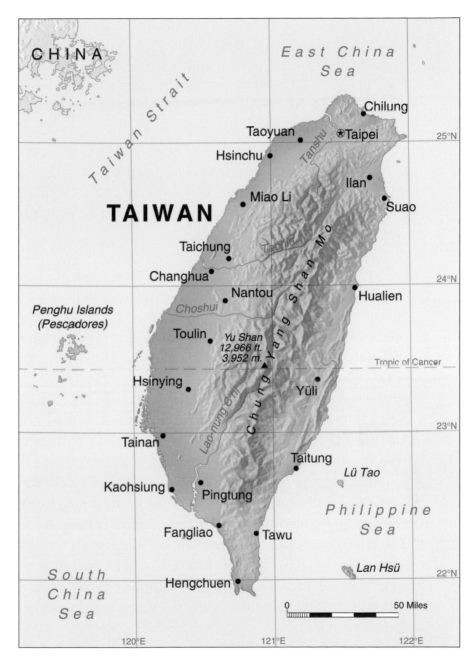

The island of Taiwan is surrounded on the west by the Taiwan Strait and on the east by the Pacific Ocean, and more than seventy-five other islands that belong to the country are scattered throughout these waters. Taiwan also has 550 miles (890 kilometers) of coastline, and over half of the island is mountainous.

The island is part of the series of arcs that march up out of insular and peninsular Southeast Asia through the Philippines, Taiwan, and the Ryukyu Islands just north of Taiwan, and then into the Japanese Archipelago. More than 75 islands are also part of Taiwan. The Pescadores Islands (the Penghu in Chinese) lie less than 50 miles (80 kilometers) west of the island. There are 64 islands in the Pescadores archipelago. The island chain has served as an important Chinese fishing base for centuries. Fifteen other islands are part of Taiwan's domain, including two small islands, Quemoy and Matsu, which lie very close to the mainland.

More than half of Taiwan is mountainous. The island's major land feature is the Central Mountain Range. This "backbone" of the island has a relatively gradual slope toward the west but a very steep escarpment (face) on the east. The abrupt eastern slope is characterized by short, fast-flowing rivers that rush onto the narrow coastal plain and on into the Pacific Ocean. Traditionally, this very steep and rugged eastern slope has been difficult to farm. As a result, few Chinese have settled the area. Because it is remote and sparsely settled, this area has become home to some of the island's remaining aboriginal populations.

In the northern part of Taiwan, there is evidence of volcanism, and throughout much of the island there are hot springs, particularly in the southeast and northeast. All of the island's volcanoes are extinct, but their presence is a reminder that Taiwan is part of the geologic "Ring of Fire" that rims the Pacific Ocean basin. Taiwan does experience earthquakes, which are also evidence of the seismic power of this Ring of Fire.

Taiwan is fortunate that the mountain slopes on the western side of the island are gentler than are those in the east. This has provided an environment suitable for more settlement and a more productive agriculture. Only about 25 percent of the island is used for farming. Much of this percentage has been

The east coast of Taiwan is characterized by rugged mountain slopes and cliffs. The photograph below shows Chingshui Cliff, one of many cliffs in this area of the island.

gained through extensive terracing (on the west, mostly) and traditionally diligent Chinese agricultural work.

The drama of this setting is given strong images in the travel book *Lonely Planet: Taiwan*:

> Shaped roughly like a leaf, the [island's] maximum length . . . is 395 km and the maximum width is 144 km . . . Though the island is small, its mountains are

extremely high, reaching 3952 m at Yushan (jade mountain), which is higher than Mt. Fuji in Japan. Indeed, outside of the Himalayas, Yushan is the highest peak in North-East Asia. The mountains rise straight out of the sea on Taiwan's east coast, while the west side of the island is a flat and fertile plain, much more hospitable to human habitation. Over 90% of Taiwan's population resides there. However, the mountainous eastern side of the island is far more scenic.

The eastern mountains lie between the cities of Hualien and Taitung on the east coast. The Taitung Mountains stretch between the two coastal cities and come down precipitously into the Pacific Ocean on their east flank. On the west flank they have helped create an 84-mile (140-kilometer)-long narrow valley. The valley has some agricultural settlement even though it is only 1–4 miles (2–7 kilometers) wide. The Taitung Mountains scarcely reach an elevation of more than 3,300 feet (1,000 meters).

Lying west of the narrow valley on the eastern edge of Taiwan is the much more massive, higher, and significant Chung Yang Shan mountain system. The Chung Yang peaks rise to nearly 10,000 feet (3,000 meters). There are, as well, more than 40 peaks that exceed 13,200 feet (4,000 meters). It is this sharp, eastward-looking face of the Chung Yang Shan that the *Lonely Planet* travel book describes as dramatic and scenic.

The Chung Yang Shan range is located off-center toward the eastern side of the island. This creates a system of relatively broad and gently sloping plains that extend toward the Taiwan Strait on the mountain system's western flank. These surfaces are reasonably well-watered and rich in alluvial (stream-deposited) soils. It is this piedmont that has been terraced for the past four centuries and that is the source of the name Taiwan, or "terraced bay." It is also on these flanks that the great majority of Taiwan's settlement, agriculture, industry, and transportation occur.

Taiwan's mountains, valleys, highland peaks, steep slopes, gentle rivers, hot springs, and wonderfully scenic landscapes are the setting for the development of one of the most important islands in Asia.

WEATHER AND CLIMATE

The Tropic of Cancer intersects Taiwan, placing the southern one-third of the island in the tropics. The overall climate pattern is one of basically two, rather than four, seasons. Summers are warm, humid, and a season of much rainfall. The average annual precipitation for the island is 102 inches (2,590 millimeters). Amounts of rainfall vary considerably, however, depending on location in relation to the Central Mountain Range. The lowlands traditionally are frost-free, but during the winter there is often snow in the high peaks of the mountains. There is also evidence of glacial history in the higher reaches of the Chung Yang Shan.

The climate engine that determines the overall pattern of rainfall is the same force that shapes much of Asia's climate— the monsoon. This pattern of seasonally reversing winds results from the fact that land and water receive, absorb, and utilize solar insolation (incoming heat from the sun) very differently. In Asia, there is a summer monsoon and a winter monsoon. The summer monsoon is of particular importance to Taiwan. It not only brings the heaviest rainfall, but it also helps spawn the typhoons that can bring such damage to the coastal regions of China, Taiwan, the Korean peninsula, Japan, and most of the islands of East Asia.

In the late spring and summer months—the high sun season—heat pours onto the land of both continental China and the island archipelagos lying to the east. As the sun's rays hit the earth's surface, the soil begins to warm, absorbing insolation during the daylight hours. By the time June and July arrive, two things begin to happen: First, the land surface grows very warm, and as this warm air rises, it cools. At the same time, relatively cooler air that is higher in pressure (lying over the ocean and seas to the east of the Asian landmass) begins to seek the areas of instability that are characterized by this low-pressure ascending air mass. Winds blow from these areas of high atmospheric pressure to regions of low atmospheric pressure.

The steady inflow of marine air masses carries moisture from the ocean onto the continent where the seasonal low-pressure zones have developed. As the moisture moves over the land, the sun bakes the continent's interior. The heating generates thermal cells of unstable hot air, causing them to rise and form massive cloud banks and often torrents of rainfall. As a result, the summer season is generally the high rainfall period in Asian climates, especially near the coast or on the windward side of mountains.

In winter, this monsoon pattern reverses. The seas and ocean are slow to give up the heat that has poured into their watery depths during the summer. The land, however, gives up the heat each night, and once the amount of insolation is greatly diminished (during the low-sun seasons of November, December, and January), the continental interior becomes the zone of cold air temperatures and relative high-pressure air masses. The ocean surface becomes, at the same time, the zone of relative low pressure because of the relative warmth still evident in this zone.

There is, however, a real difference in the impact this reverse monsoon airflow generates. The summer monsoons are full of moisture and bring rain to often parched landscapes. In the winter, however, a reverse pattern develops, with air blowing from interior Asia outward toward the sea. There is little moisture in this eastward airflow; hence, there is much less precipitation. Only on the windward slopes of high

Taiwan's climate features warm, rainy summers and cold, mostly dry winters. The region also frequently suffers from damaging monsoons and typhoons. Here, a family tries to navigate down a flooded street in a suburb of Taipei after typhoon Herb in July 1996.

mountain ranges is air forced up high enough to condense and allow precipitation to occur.

For Taiwan, this monsoon pattern provides the island with its greatest amounts of precipitation during the summer. A characteristic daily pattern is (1) the slow buildup of heat during the day; (2) by mid- to late afternoon, the rising of warm air, allowing the air to cool and moisture to condense, forming huge clouds; (3) brief summer thundershowers lasting no more than a few minutes to perhaps one hour or more; and (4) a drying period following the rainfall, during which the air is cooler, and the evening relatively pleasant. The entire process begins again with the return of the intense sun's rays the next day.

Typhoons are another aspect of the climate pattern of Taiwan. During the summer months the monsoon influences can create enormously powerful, intense tropical storms. These storms, called hurricanes in the Western Hemisphere, are called typhoons in the western Pacific Ocean. The word comes from the Chinese term *da feng* (great wind). These storms pound the coasts of continental Asia and the island margins of the Philippines, Taiwan, the Korean peninsula, and the Japanese archipelago. Such typhoons cause floods and washouts, bring monumental winds and thunderstorms, and result in great damage to both settled urban areas and croplands in these places. Taiwan is struck by an average of three to four typhoons annually, most often in the late summer.

The climate of Taiwan is also influenced by the Kuroshio Current. This warm current is sometimes described as the counterpart to the Gulf Stream–North Atlantic Drift that brings relative warmth to western Europe. It begins in the tropics and flows poleward, flowing both east and west of Taiwan. The combination of that current and the pattern of monsoon winds gives Taiwan a warm climate with hot summers, high humidity—especially on the lowlands of the western coastal plain—and a precipitation pattern influenced also by orographic features in the Chung Yang Shan.

As will be seen later, this climate pattern allows two harvests of rice—the major food crop—a year in most places. In the tropical southwest, even three crops can be grown and harvested each year. The major problem with Taiwan's climate is that the winter monsoon brings too little rain in the lowlands and the island is sometimes described as suffering from a winter drought.

PLANTS AND ANIMALS

Nearly two-thirds of Taiwan is forested. Geographer Albert Kolb describes the island's vegetation in these terms:

> The low-lying tropical woodlands have been largely felled since the seventeenth century and 43 percent of this land is now cultivated, interspersed with airy groups of acacias or bamboo thickets. Mangrove swamps occupy some of the tidal deltaic southern coastline. At higher levels only 2 percent of the land is under cultivation. Subtropical forests of broad-leaved evergreens (oak and laurel forest) flourish between altitudes of 300 m (1000 ft) and 500 m (1600 ft) in the north, and between 600 m (2000 ft) and 2000 m (6500 ft) in the south, immediately above the rainforest of the lowland. Here one finds Chinese cork oaks and up to about 1500 m (5000 ft) camphor trees, much valued for their sap and wood. Above this stage, up to about 2600 m (8000 ft) there is mixed forest, mostly evergreen and deciduous oaks, deciduous maples, elms and beeches, with some pines. Conifer forests extend between 2600 m (8000 ft) and 3600 m (12000 ft) and on the heights above one finds dwarf pines and cushion plants.

The rainforest lands have been almost all completely replaced by settlement and cropland. The biotic resource base is ever smaller as settlement and development for the increasingly important tourist industry expand up the slopes of the western flank of the central mountains. In eastern Taiwan, the forests have been less disturbed. Here, the island's patterns of growth have been less intense. Also, the government has worked to preserve the more agriculturally marginal landscapes of eastern Taiwan in light of Asian tourism to the region's scenic mountains, hot springs, and mountain stream systems.

In terms of vertical zonation, Taiwan's plant inventory looks like this:

- 0–2,000 feet (0–600 meters): mostly bamboo, palms, and tropical evergreens.

- 2,000–6,000 feet (600–1,800 meters): subtropical evergreen forests, camphor, and laurel.

- 6,000–8,000 feet (1,800–7,200 meters): broad-leaved evergreen forests of the Asian temperate zone with cedars, cypress, junipers, rhododendrons, maples, *cryptomeria* (Japanese cedar).

The fauna of the island bears great resemblance to the pattern of south China. Deer, wild boars, bears, monkeys, goats, wildcats, and panthers are the animals that show up in inventories, but it is important to realize that these animals are living in the less disturbed forest lands, and particularly in the regions at higher elevations. There are also mongooses, foxes, and 220 native bird species.

In Taiwan, only the upland aboriginal people still practice hunting as part of their life pattern. The increasing spread of settlement and the expanding network of transportation links have diminished the richness of the island's fauna. Animals that once roamed the land are slowly being

Nearly two-thirds of Taiwan is forested, and pristine mountains, green fields and wildlife are often just a few miles outside of major cities. In this photograph a water buffalo rests in a mud puddle while hikers follow a nearby trail in Yangmingshan National Park.

replaced with agricultural terraces, hot springs, mountain resort facilities, and local peoples' decreasing interest in wildlife. During recent decades, there has been some effort to slow the rate of loss of local fauna. This movement is related to the growth of the tourist industry, including rapidly growing ecotourism.

MINERALS

Historically, Taiwan has had a good resource base that has included coal, limestone, marble, natural gas, and forest products. However, the success with which Taiwan has educated, trained, and managed its human resources has resulted in a work force more involved in economic endeavors than in cultivating the country's natural resources. Coal has steadily decreased in importance because of the growing use of natural gas and petroleum fuel and the associated decline of coal value. Between 1989 and 1993, for example, the export value of both coal and natural gas dropped by approximately 50 percent, yet the island's economy was growing at between 8 and 11 percent annually. Such a statistic should remind us all that resources take on value only within the context in which they are found. Resources have value in direct relationship to their setting, the contemporary timeframe, and the level of economic development overall. For Taiwan, the resources of growing significance over the past three decades have been human skills development and political-economic organization—at both the local and global levels.

Even so, limestone has been a very important building resource. Marble has been mined as a building rock. It also has generated considerable income as a craft material in the creation of Taiwan handicrafts from eastern Taiwan river gorges and tourist centers.

The presence of this handsome rock resource in the deeply cut river gorges, coupled with the traditional presence of the aboriginal population in eastern Taiwan, has given the island a distinctive polarity in land use. On the western side of Taiwan are the major settlements, the most productive croplands, and the most highly developed transportation network. On the eastern side of the island, the landscape is less well developed, but provides a dramatic tourist resource.

The very modest role of minerals and their economic importance is illustrated by the fact that, in 2002, less than one-half of 1 percent of the country's gross national product (GNP) came from mining. In terms of labor, only 11,000 people are employed in mineral extraction, whereas some 2,600,000 are involved in manufacturing. Taiwan has moved well beyond the export of primary resources as a major economic activity. The resources that are most dominant in the island's economy center on the productive use of skilled labor and nonmineral-based industry.

3

Historical Geography

An island is a special world. It has a naturally defined "edge." Particularly if it is a relatively small island, it is a place in which a person can better manage to understand the various conditions and historical events that have shaped that space. And if that island lies along a pathway of commerce or exploration, it develops into an even more special world because of its history and maritime traditions. Taiwan's history has been powerfully shaped by just such a location.

As mentioned earlier, Taiwan is part of the chain of large and small islands that course down from the Aleutian Islands through the Japanese archipelago and the Ryukyu chain. The string continues southward through the Philippines and into the complex of islands and peninsulas that make up Southeast Asia. This all is part of the Ring of Fire. It is also a corridor that has been used as a migration pathway for tens of thousands of years.

Migrating groups generally have come to Taiwan from the Southeast Asia region. These groups have, through the centuries, migrated northward, with various populations selecting specific locales to settle along the way. Through time, various migrating groups have permanently settled all of the major islands they have encountered.

ORIGINAL SETTLERS

Before the Chinese became interested in the island of Taiwan in the sixteenth and seventeenth centuries, the island was occupied by aboriginal stock from Indonesia that settled the western sloping flanks and even the steeply ridged eastern region. According to Michael Stainton, one of the authors included in Murray Rubenstein's edited work, *Taiwan: A New History*:

> There are today at least 380,000 people in Taiwan, now officially called "Taiwan Aboriginal Peoples," who are speakers of Austronesian languages. Their dozen extant, and dozen extinct, languages are agreed to be the most archaic of the Indonesian branch (at least) of that vast language family. Their cultures and physical attributes, which are quite varied, also identify them as Austronesian peoples. There have been human settlements [in Taiwan] since at least fifteen thousand years ago, in the palaeolithic age. By the seventeenth century there were several ethno-linguistically distinct groups settled in Taiwan.

There has been much argument in scholarly circles about the exact origins of the *kao-shan tzu* (high mountain people), as the aborigines are generally called. However, most believe their presence on Taiwan is related to the steady migration of Austronesian or Malayo-Polynesian peoples northward from the South Pacific region and Southeast Asia.

There is a political dimension to the discussions about the origins and presence of these several hundred thousand people in

The original inhabitants of Taiwan were aborigines from Indonesia who lost their land when other settlers from all over the world came to the island. Recently, the native people have organized into political groups and started movements to regain their own land. These aborigine children from the Paiwan tribe wear traditional costumes and play during a harvest festival.

Taiwan. In 1988, there was, for the first time, a mobilization of the aboriginal people. This was called the "Return Our Land" movement and the movement organizers issued this statement:

The Aboriginal People of Taiwan ("Mountain People") are the first people to have lived on this island of Taiwan. Because of this, our right to the land is absolute and a priori. Those lands which have been robbed by violence or deceit by the later occupying Han Chinese, or taken by successive governments by legal force, should by right be returned to us. (Stainton in Rubenstein)

There was participation in a UN Working Group on Indigenous Populations that same year, and by mid-1991, the "Return Our Land" movement had become the "Aboriginal Constitutional Movement." This was virtually the first time that the indigenous people of Taiwan had become represented in any sort of political movement that spoke to their status and their desire for their own land.

In 1993, a man from the Ami Tribe—a tribe concentrated in the more remote eastern Taiwan mountain regions—presented a paper in Beijing at a sociology symposium. His name was Tsai Chung-han. He held a doctorate in sociology from Tokyo University and was a native of Taitung, the major city of southeastern Taiwan.

Dr. Tsai's theme was that the Ami and other aboriginal people of Taiwan had not come from the Asian mainland. Using linguistic and archaeological evidence, he refuted such claims and concluded his paper saying:

If the proto-Austronesian peoples came from mainland China, how is it that today in China there is not a single Austronesian people? Ethnic migration is essentially an expansion, and not a matter of the entire group departing from its ancestral territory. In the whole world there is no example of any such ethnic migration. (Stainton in Rubenstein)

Thus, it is most likely that the island was first settled, as mentioned earlier, by an erratic but continuing migration of peoples from the south. It is believed that, beginning as early as

15,000 years ago, they moved northward into lands less settled than those from which they came.

CHINESE SETTLERS IN TAIWAN

The Chinese province of Fujian (historically Fukien) lies across the Taiwan Strait from Taiwan. This province has been the most significant source of Chinese migrants to the island. Fujian has a very mountainous landscape (although without any peaks as high as the tallest mountain in Taiwan) and settlement is largely concentrated on the coastal lowlands at the eastern edge of the province. According to a Chinese saying: "Fujian is 80 percent mountains, 10 percent water, and 10 percent farming."

This area was settled late by the Han Chinese. The difficulty of establishing a road link across Fujian's mountains to the East China Sea made connections difficult. Moreover, malaria posed a problem in the province's coastal lowlands and marshes. It was the classic frontier riddle: How does a country find the money to drain wetlands and build cities before people move into the area?

In the case of China, Fujian, and Taiwan, the riddle was answered by a shift in government policy during the Sung dynasty (960–1279) that placed new emphasis on this southeastern coastal region. During that period much attention was given to draining the coastal marshes. Paradoxically, attention also was given to the construction of major irrigation networks that utilized water from streams flowing down Fujian's mountain slopes. The water was used to flood new rice fields that supported a growing Chinese agricultural population. Coastal villages grew into fishing ports and population began to expand with a new vitality.

With a change in government during the 1430s, China suddenly ended the wide-ranging naval explorations that had characterized the first three decades of the fifteenth century—nearly a century before Columbus took his three ships across the Atlantic—and supported the burgeoning population in Fujian province. Up to this point China had the most ambitious and effective naval force in the world. In what are called the Ming Voyages, Admiral Cheng Ho captained seven major voyages to the south and west of China mostly under Emperor Yung Lo. These voyages involved major ships with crews numbering as many as 400 men. According to historical documents, they sailed to places west of the Indian subcontinent into the Arabian Gulf, around the Horn of Africa, and down the northeast coast of Africa all the way to Mombassa in today's Kenya.

In the 1930s a new Ming dynastic court in Beijing declared it illegal to launch such distant voyages and, soon thereafter, disallowed anything beyond coastal fishing in the waters of the Taiwan Strait and East China Sea. Such a change in the rules of access to the sea brought a great hardship on the new populations that had grown up along the Fujian coast and in its villages that looked out on the channel of water separating the mainland from the terraced mountain slopes of Taiwan. It was during this time period that a steady stream of Chinese began migrating to Taiwan.

THE PORTUGUESE AND TAIWAN

In 1590 the Portuguese "discovered" Taiwan and named the island "Ilha Formosa," or Beautiful Island. Although they made some weak attempts to settle the island, they failed to gain a foothold there. Instead, the Portuguese focused their attention on the Chinese mainland, particularly the harbor at the mouth of the Xi River and the Pearl River Delta. Here, they established Macao in 1577. That city and British-controlled Hong Kong, both of which are in the same delta region, were the only two Chinese ports open to European trade until the 1842 conclusion of the Opium War between China and Great Britain.

SEVENTEENTH-CENTURY INTERESTS IN TAIWAN

In 1624, the Dutch settled two towns in southwestern Taiwan. Zeelandia (now Anping) was first settled as a fort in 1624, and Provintia (now Tainan) was established as an administrative center in 1653. These two towns were the focus of efforts by the Dutch East India Company to colonize the island. This foreign settlement was the only one to last for any period of time in Taiwan until the 50 years of Japanese control from 1895–1945. The arrival of the Dutch also brought the first presence of Christianity to the island.

The Dutch were initially followed by the Spanish, who, in 1626, settled in the harbor area of northeastern Taiwan, in what today is called Keelung. Their efforts to establish a viable settlement there also heralded the arrival of Roman Catholicism in Taiwan. Spanish influence on the island was short-lived, however. By the early 1640s, the Dutch had forced the Spanish out of any island role. The Spanish thereby were denied any stronghold north of the Philippines, where they focused most of their East Asian colonial efforts.

In the final decades of the Ming dynasty (early 1600s), some estimated 25,000 to 100,000 Chinese peasants from Fujian province, and perhaps from adjacent provinces of the Chinese coast, set sail for Taiwan. The island was seen as virgin land even though there had been some Chinese immigration there prior to the period of chaos between the ruling Chinese and the invading Manchus (discussed in more detail later) that occurred from the 1620s to the 1650s. By the 1650s, the Dutch were actively promoting Chinese migration to Taiwan. They hoped to harness the energy of Chinese farmers in such a way that the Dutch East India Company could produce a reliable agricultural surplus for trade and export.

In their effort to bolster their control of Taiwan from the 1640s onward, the Dutch made land, seed, farm implements, and money available to all Chinese peasants who came across the Taiwan Strait and opened new farm fields. Their settlement efforts were focused along the southwest coast cities of (present-day) Anping and Tainan, which were located just south of the Tropic of Cancer. They also undertook the development of irrigation and water control projects. Crops promoted by the Dutch for their trade needs included rice, tea, sugar cane, hemp, and wheat. These were all crops with which the Chinese migrants had experience—or were at least acquainted with from local farming patterns in the Fujian provincial landscape.

The Dutch East India Company—founded in 1602 and viable until the end of the eighteenth century—was focused on global trade with the Spice Islands, all lying south of Taiwan. Although Taiwan was never central to spice trade traffic in East Asia, the Dutch still held an interest in the island during the mid-seventeenth century. The company had, after all, profited immensely from the spice trade in Southeast Asia and from marketing to the European world. A twist on this Taiwan development effort is noted by geographer Ron Knapp:

> An effort was made [by the Dutch] to survey the island and to make maps, but most mapmakers captured no more than the mere outline of the island without the details of its filling in by Chinese pioneers. Seven seventeenth-century European sketch maps gave cartographic definition to the island. Yet, in accentuating how limited the Dutch colony was, they revealed their obliviousness to the extent of Chinese settlement by showing most of the island as unexplored and uninhabited. Even European maps of the eighteenth century still failed to capture the spread of Chinese settlement, which by then had become considerable. (Knapp in Rubenstein)

Dutch rule ended in 1664, however, at which time the number of Dutch colonials living on the island amounted to only 2,800, 2,200 of whom were soldiers. Although the Dutch were gone some four decades after their initial settlement of Zeelandia, this fort and palisade complex merged with Tainan, creating the island's most substantial city until the end of the nineteenth century.

The primary force that removed the Dutch from Taiwan and contributed to an increased flow of Chinese migrants to the island was the Chinese military man Cheng Ch'eng-kung, or Koxinga, as he is named in Western histories of the period. At the end of the Ming dynasty, the Chinese undertook an ambitious campaign to keep China from falling under the control of the foreign Manchus. Manchus were a people of the plains and forests located north of China proper, in what has generally been called Manchuria. They were not welcomed by the Chinese in any way.

Koxinga, of Chinese-Japanese parentage, was a powerful warlord, and is seen as the most powerful general in this mid-seventeenth-century era of disintegrating Chinese control. He established a base in the Tainan area of Taiwan in anticipation of using the island as a base for better control of the mainland Here he tried to organize a force to thwart the arrival of the Manchus in China. Also, he encouraged the Chinese arriving in Taiwan to go inland from the coastal areas where they had been settling during the prior 20–40 years. In this effort, some 37 new Chinese settlements were established and Chinese control and development of the southwestern coastal plain and piedmont landscapes of the western side of the island was achieved by the 1680s.

It is estimated that by the 1680s some 100,000–150,000 Han Chinese had come to and settled on the island. The death of Koxinga and the relatively weak continuation of his regime in the early 1680s, however, allowed the Manchus to gain full control of Taiwan by 1683. The Manchus had now gained

Throughout its history, Taiwan has constantly suffered from occupation and meddling by other countries. In the seventeenth century, the Dutch and the Chinese had the most involvement in Taiwan. This photograph shows a statue of Chinese General Koxinga, looking out over China's ancient port city of Xiamen. Koxinga's victory over Dutch forces on Taiwan paved the way for increased Chinese migration to and control over Taiwan.

control of all of China, and the Manchu Ch'ing dynasty began a period of rule that lasted until 1911.

One of the most distinct peoples to migrate to Taiwan during the seventeenth century were the Hakka, who had become a significant mountain population in Kwangtung province in southeast China. These people, also known as the "guest people," were a minority population among the Han Chinese and were more comfortable seeking remote upland environments for their nucleated settlements. They also became known as a strong fighting group in the decades of Ch'ing control of the island. The Hakka continued to maintain a strong collective identity during the steady growth of the island in the eighteenth and nineteenth centuries.

The Hakka were the population most willing to harvest and process camphor from the densely wooded uplands of the western side of the Chung Yang Shan. The camphor trees (*Cinnamomum camphora*) were cut down and hacked into chips, and the chips were distilled right on the spot to extract the oil. At the time, there was no substitute for the special qualities of camphor oil taken from the camphor tree. It has valuable use as a stimulant, a medicine, an inhalant, and as an additive to the making of lacquer ware, an important craft trade of both China and Japan. The harvesting process was made more difficult by the fact that the camphor trees tended to be in the forest lands of the aboriginal peoples of upland Taiwan—some of these peoples continued their traditional head-hunting customs right into the nineteenth century!

TAIWAN IN THE NINETEENTH CENTURY

At the time of the first Sino-British war (1839), also known as the Opium War, Taiwan had a population of approximately 2,500,000. By that time rice and sugar had become agricultural surpluses that played a strong trade role between the island and the Chinese mainland. In what is sometimes called the second Opium War (1858), the British forced the Chinese to open additional main-land Chinese ports to foreign trade. The two ports of Tainan and Tamshui (on the northwest corner of Taiwan) were included in this 1858 Treaty Port provision. This brought the island into its fullest economic link yet with the mainland.

In addition to the major waves of migration to Taiwan during the dynasty transition of the mid-seventeenth century, the nineteenth century saw another major increase in the flow of migrants. The Taiping Rebellion (1850–1864) was a major effort by Chinese to unseat the Ch'ing (Manchu) dynasty. It occurred during the period of Taiwan's increasing economic importance to China and was centered around the provinces on the mainland's coast and at the mouth of the Yangtze River, with Nanking (Nanjing) being taken and established as capital for the rebellion in 1853. It is estimated that nearly 20 million Chinese died during this 15-year period of hostility. The chaos resulting from these battles once again caused many coastal Chinese to flee to the relatively safe haven of Taiwan.

In 1874, the Japanese launched a military campaign against southern Taiwan in an effort to pull China into a Sino-Japanese conflict. A decade later, the French blockaded the major northern ports of Taiwan and the Penghu Islands (also called the Pescadores from the early Portuguese influence). Although neither of these efforts was successful, the Chinese mainland government could see the emerging importance of Taiwan. In 1885 the island was, for the first time, given full provincial status. This, according to Robert Gardella, a specialist in Chinese business history, led to:

> Vigorous efforts . . . to enhance frontiers via Han Chinese colonization and aboriginal "pacification," and [the introduction of] strategically significant elements of Western technology and techniques (i.e., military hardware, a railroad, indigenous steamship services, modern mining, telegraphic links to the mainland, a modern postal service). Striking as they appear in the late Ch'ing context, these innovations and reforms were simply unequal to the larger task of ensuring Taiwan's political fate in the jungle of the *fin de siècle* East Asian power politics. (Gardella in Rubenstein)

THE SINO-JAPANESE WAR AND TAIWAN AS A JAPANESE COLONY

The Japanese were victorious, however, in another conflict with China, the cost of which was very high for China. As mentioned earlier, Japan had attempted to gain access to ports and some authority in Taiwan for decades. The island's sugar production, in particular, was of major importance to Japan. Japan's smashing victory in the 1894–1895 Sino-Japanese War allowed the victors to claim the entire island as a war prize. Japanese rule was imposed upon Taiwan by China's agreement to the Treaty of Shimonoseki (1895). This treaty granted the island to the Japanese and represented an action completely beyond the control of the Chinese population on Taiwan. The island began its Japanese colonial history just as it was becoming a significant player in China trade. This same loss for China also forced the Ch'ing dynasty to grant Japan rights in China that put Japan on a par with the Western countries that were militarily and economically active in East Asia. China also suffered an enormous loss of face in being defeated by the small island empire that lay off its northeast coast. Of course, this shift brought major changes for Taiwan.

By 1905 there were nearly 60,000 Japanese in Taiwan. By 1935, the number had grown to more than 270,000 out of a total Taiwan population of about 6,500,000. In August 1945, the island's Japanese colonial government was astonished at the abruptness of the Japanese uncon-ditional surrender to the Allies, effectively ending World War II. This forced the repatriation of all of the Japanese on Taiwan to their home country and the return to Taiwan of more than 200,000 Taiwanese who had been involved in the war effort, including 80,433 servicemen and 126,750 civilians.

Nevertheless, significant economic and social innova-tions were introduced in Taiwan during the Japanese colonial period. An extensive network of rail lines and roadways was laid down in western Taiwan. By 1935, there were more than 7,000 factories on the island, generally small-scale shops. By mid-1943, the number of skilled laborers had grown to 147,000, and the total number of nonagricultural workers (male and female) who worked in mining, transportation, communications, and other services had risen to more than 200,000. This shift was significant because prior to the arrival of the Japanese, Taiwan's economy had largely centered on agricultural production; most of the goods that were shipped were raw or semiprocessed agricultural products. (The fact that an estimated 80,000 Taiwanese Chinese were in the Japanese army at the end of the war further illustrates Japan's influence on the island during its years of colonial dominance.)

By the mid-1940s, a labor force of some 200,000 people was engaged in construction and other military-related employment. As the Japanese commitment in the Pacific war expanded, Taiwan increased its role in specialized industrial activities. One important contribution was the continued distillation of camphor oil for export to Japan. The construction of military airports on Taiwan was another. As a result of this expanded industrial activity, by the end of World War II many Taiwanese had gained vocational and even some managerial experience in nonagricultural positions. The importance of these developments to Taiwan is discussed in considerable detail in the chapters on government and economy.

POST–WORLD WAR II MIGRATION PATTERNS

The last great migration flow to Taiwan came in the middle of the twentieth century when between 1,800,000 and 2,000,000 Chinese Nationalist military men and their families fled the mainland as the forces of Chiang Kai-shek's Kuomintang (KMT) were collapsing in the Chinese Civil

War, taking with them enormous collections of art and material goods.

In 1945, before this migration, Taiwan had a population of approximately 6,500,000; a decade later the island's population had grown to more than 9,000,000. This population increase is not necessarily monumental in numbers, but in political, social, and economic importance it meant a great deal, since the Taiwanese population at the end of World War II had just endured 50 years of Japanese colonial rule.

As the Japanese surrendered, the forces of domination on Taiwan again shifted, in ways that again had no political regard for the Taiwanese population on the island. As the armies of Chiang Kai-shek became weaker and lost more ground, the Nationalists began to look for a strategic base at which they could regroup in order to make a later attempt at defeat of the Chinese Communists. So, as had been the case with Koxinga in the 1660s, Taiwan was again seen as a haven. A military shift from the mainland to Taiwan began as early as 1946 and 1947, with the major KMT migration occurring between 1948 and 1950.

Control of the new government slipped out of the hands of the Taiwanese as the migrating Nationalists rapidly emerged as the new social and political power brokers and economic upper class. The KMT worked quickly to consolidate the industrial and institutional gains that had been achieved by the Japanese. By the time of the Nationalist defeat on the mainland—October 1, 1949—control of Taiwan was already in the hands of the KMT. They were assisted by many Chinese Taiwanese who were eager to accommodate them in hope of soon realizing their dream of returning to the mainland.

By the end of the twentieth century, the population of Taiwan had grown to approximately 22,000,000. In the next chapter we will look at the demographic characteristics and distribution of this population. As you anticipate such a discussion, remember that the Taiwan population amounts to well less than 1 percent of the population of mainland China, yet these 22,000,000-plus people have developed a dimension of importance that indeed makes them members of a "parallel universe" in relation to the mainland.

CHAPTER

4

People and Culture

POPULATION DYNAMICS IN TAIWAN

Consider the pattern of Taiwan population growth that is shown in the following table. This island is approximately one-fifth the size of Missouri, yet it has a total population approximately five times greater than that state's. Taiwan serves as a tiny microcosm of mainland China in many ways. Its patterns of population development will help you better understand the character of the island and why this book suggests that Taiwan is a "parallel universe" of China.

POPULATION GROWTH

The periods of most dramatic population growth in Taiwan have been linked with periods of major migration from the Chinese mainland. This pattern was particularly significant in the years following World War II and with the initial arrival of the 1,800,000

Table 1. Taiwan Population Growth

DATE	POPULATION
1684	100,000
1839	2,500,000
1905	3,039,000
1915	3,400,000
1925	4,000,000
1935	5,200,000
1945	6,500,000
1955	9,000,000
1965	12,600,000
1975	16,100,000
1985	19,200,000
1995	21,300,000
2002	22,500,000

Sources: Adapted from Knapp in Rubenstein, and *Encyclopedia Britannica Book of the Year*, selected years.

to 2,000,000 KMT Chinese during the late 1940s. The 1950s were tense because of China's continual threat to cross the Taiwan Strait and make a military effort to reclaim the province of Taiwan as part of the Chinese body politic. That tension was eased somewhat by the fact that the United States decided to include Taiwan as part of the world protected by the U.S. Seventh Fleet that patrolled the China Sea, Sea of Japan, and waters lying off the east of the East Asia mainland. All these events had an impact on the population growth of the island.

The most remarkable aspect of Taiwan's population pattern is the sharp decline in the rate of growth that occurred during and following the 1960s. The average rate of natural increase (RNI), defined in more detail later, in the late 1950s and the early 1960s was greater than 2 percent annually. The KMT government—assisted by both governmental programs and nongovernmental organizations—began to work actively to reduce Taiwan's rate of population growth. Taiwan's leaders saw that the great majority of the economic and social outcomes of improved planning and increased productivity would be consumed by the potential doubling of the island's population in 20 to 30 years. This meant that many of the benefits of good planning would be lost to rapid population increase.

By 1975, the rate of growth had dropped to below 2.0 percent and by 1986 it was 1.4 percent. It continued to drop and by 2003 it had declined to 0.6 percent, a level comparable to that of the United States. This has been one of the most dramatic declines in birthrate of any place in the developing world in the past half century. It has been of major importance in allowing the country's economy to develop. In fact, Taiwan's economy has moved into the full-fledged role of a More Developed Country (MDC). In East Asia, it has become one of the economic success stories and is labeled as one of the "East Asian Dragons," or "Four Tigers," which also includes South Korea, Singapore, and Hong Kong.

A very close link exists between population growth and economic development. If population grows at a rate greater than that of economic growth, the country suffers. If, on the other hand, the economy grows at a rate faster than the population, it can reap the rewards of its efforts toward economic development. In attempting to develop economically, for example, a country might invest huge sums of money in highways, airports, and education. Improvement in these areas are the hallmarks of modernization and economic growth. If, however, population growth outstrips economic

Despite its small size, Taiwan has a population of more than twenty-two million. This photograph shows one of many streets crowded with cars, businesses, and people in Taipei, the capital of Taiwan.

development and the country continually has fewer jobs for its people (especially young people) who are eager to work, then frustration grows. If a job shortage is accompanied by a food shortage, then no matter what effort is dedicated to development, there is little sense of any national accomplishment.

For those reasons, one of the most effective things a country can do to modernize is to help reduce the rate of natural increase (RNI) of the population. Taiwan has been enormously effective in its attempts to achieve this change. Table 2 compares Taiwan's statistics in this area with averages for East Asia and for the world as a whole. This simple comparison clearly shows that the island has become a model of population management. Such success enables the country to devote more capital and intellectual energy to the complex process of continued modernization and economic development.

Let's consider the impact of each of these population characteristics in the shaping of the personality of the whole country.

Total Population

When considered in terms of population density, population growth rate, and levels of education, population magnitude becomes a major factor in a country's social as well as economic potential. Table 1 shows the longer term growth pattern of Taiwan's population. Although its population is small, even tiny, compared to the 1.3 billion of mainland China, it is still large enough to give the island a population density of 1,600 people per square mile (620 square kilometers). This is approximately five times that of China, and more than twenty times that of the United States.

Birthrate

Taiwan's 11 per 1,000 birthrate is about two-thirds that of East Asia's average, and just about one-half the world average. Effecting a change in a country's birthrate is a much more difficult and slow-moving process than changing the death rate (number of deaths per 1,000 people). Public health measures such as inoculation rates, number of clinics, and increase in food availability all have a positive impact on the death rate, making the lowering of that rate easier to achieve through, for

Table 2. Taiwan Population Characteristics Compared with East Asia and the World

CHARACTERISTIC	TAIWAN RATE	E. ASIA RATE	WORLD RATE
Population:	22,500,000		
Births per 1,000 people annually	11	15	21
Deaths per 1,000 people annually	6	7	9
Rate of Natural Increase (RNI)	0.6	0.7	1.3
Projected 2050 population total	25,200,000		
Infant mortality rate per 1,000	6.1	29	54
Percent of population <15 years	21	22	30
Percent of population >65 years	9	8	7
Life expectancy at birth (avg.)	75	72	67
Percent of population urban	77	44	47
GNI PPP*	$12,941	$6,280	$7,140

Sources: 2002 World Population Data Sheet, Population Reference Bureau; *Encyclopedia Britannica Book of the Year, 2002.*

* Gross National Income in Purchasing Power Parity

example, technology transfer. But to change the birthrate, there generally has to be a fundamental change in the way of thinking of the population that is between the ages of 18 and 45.

In Taiwan in the 1960s, the government became interested in trying to modify family patterns. A number of agencies and organizations (both governmental and nongovernmental) began to introduce concepts of family planning that would enable parents to have children when they chose to rather than when it just "happened." Family planning programs were not intended to eliminate family growth altogether, but to allow growth to take place when the parents were better able to plan and afford it.

The urbanization of Taiwan had an impact on the country's birthrate as well. Generally, urban residents tend to have fewer children than do rural families. More than 75 percent of all Taiwanese live in cities, representing one of the highest rates of urban living in all of Asia.

In Taiwan, the change in RNI became more apparent in the 1970s, and the movement toward the island's current low levels of growth really began in that decade. Taiwan has achieved one of the lowest birthrates in Asia.

Death Rate

Improved public health, better transportation, and growth in the number of hospitals and medical personnel—all are factors that help to reduce a country's death rate. Taiwan's death rate—the number of deaths per 1,000 population per year—reflects a changing countryside and marked transformation of a national demographic pattern. As a result of its dramatic success in economic development during the final four decades of the twentieth century, Taiwan was able to bring its death rate to its current very low rate of 6 per 1,000 annually. In addition, Taiwan's literacy rate has been high for the last 60 years. This has also been a major factor in reducing the death rate, because the higher the level of education, the longer the life expectancy; hence, the lower the death rate.

Rate of Natural Increase (RNI)

The number of deaths subtracted from the number of live births (both per 1,000 people) in a given year provides the Rate of Natural Increase (RNI). For Taiwan this comes to 0.6, one of the lowest rates in Asia. When you recall that Taiwan had an RNI of more than 2.0 just half a century ago, this shift is monumental. Such a change reflects governmental efficiency, levels of literacy, and both national and global efforts to bring world population growth under control. Taiwan has benefited from its own success in both economic development and standard of living. It also has been used as a model for other countries trying to lower their birthrates and RNIs.

Projected 2050 Population Total

The data appearing in Table 1 show a very low rate of population growth in Taiwan during recent decades. Growth is projected to continue at a very low rate over the next five decades. In fact, Taiwan's 2050 population is expected to be only 25,200,000, a gain of only 2.7 million. By comparison, Iraq has 23.5 million and its projected population in 2050 is 60 million; Malaysia's population of 24.4 million is expected to increase to 46.4 million; Pakistan is projected to increase from 250 million to 350 million by 2050. It can be seen that the impact of a lower RNI has enormous implications for many aspects of future development.

Infant Mortality

The infant mortality rate in Taiwan is 6.1 per 1,000. This compares to 29 for East Asia and 54 for the world as a whole. Again, Taiwan's remarkably low infant mortality rate can be attributed to effective public health programs, literacy rates, and medical facilities, and an overall high level of good health. Comparable rates are 8 for South Korea and an average of 5 for northern Europe, but an average of 97 for eastern Africa and 29 in South America. The rate in the United States is 6.6 and in Canada, 5.3. Taiwan has achieved a remarkable index as a result of all of the energy and support it has given population control and public health since the end of World War II.

Percent of Population Under 15 Years of Age

Why is this number so significant? First, this is the age group that most needs access to educational facilities. Second, it is also this cohort (age group) that will be looking for jobs in the relatively near future. Third, this is the group that soon will begin to form families of their own. More than a fifth of Taiwan's population is in this category. This is one of the reasons that the island government has been so attentive to the development of educational institutions at all levels during the past three decades, and it has been particularly effective in accommodating educational needs. This decision was made because the country decided to link its whole program of economic development to the growth of high technology. Such an economic sector can only succeed when it is nested in a country with very strong educational standards and institutions.

Thoughtful institutional planning, robust economic activity, and the social well-being of a country's population are keys to a country's success. Their implementation and success depend upon careful planning and a sound and stable government. Such a process begins, in good part, with accommodating the needs of the under-15 cohort of the population. Taiwan has been particularly attentive to this pattern.

Percent of Population Over 65 Years of Age

Taiwan's medical successes have had a major impact on the steady growth of the over-65 age cohort. Those who are over 65 years old in a general sense are dependent upon others. They have, in most cases, completed their working lives and, with good health and a resulting relatively long life expectancy, they become a population that needs shelter, medical and societal support, and perhaps even additional economic opportunities.

The under-15 and over-65 sectors of the population combine to form what is called the Dependency Ratio of a country's population. The very young who are not yet working and the senior citizens who have, in most cases, completed their working lives are dependent upon the working population between the ages of 15 and 65.

There is another dimension that gives importance to the over-65 cohort of Taiwan's population. In traditional Chinese society, the senior population is a central part of the extended family, particularly in the rural setting. Rural households often have three generations living under one roof. Homes often expand in size to accommodate grandparents, or even uncles and aunts. This means that the so-called safety net for traditional seniors in Chinese society is made up of younger family members, many of whom share the same farmstead.

Recently, however, this pattern has been changing profoundly, as many of Taiwan's rural people have moved to the city. In urban spaces, it is more difficult to accommodate the senior family folk without extra expense. At the same time, family patterns are changing and younger families seem to be less interested in having grandparents living with them. This means that the senior-citizen factor in the Dependency Ratio now requires a wholly different and innovative social framework in Taiwan society.

Average Life Expectancy at Birth

The average life expectancy in Taiwan, like so many other indices, illustrates the advanced level of development that the country has achieved. Taiwan has a combined (male and female) average life expectancy of 76 years. To have an average age expectancy that is nearly ten years beyond the world average (67) and five years more than the regional average demonstrates the high level of medical care and quality of life that is characteristic of Taiwan. In terms of longevity, in fact, Taiwan compares favorably to much of Europe.

Percent Urban Population

As mentioned earlier, approximately 77 percent of all Taiwanese live in urban areas. This number compares with the world average of just under 50 percent. In eastern Asia, only 44 percent of the population is urban. Taiwan is one of the most heavily urbanized populations in the region.

Why does this matter? Why is having an urban population important? In fact, everything about this statistic is significant. To a geographer, it is one of the most important of all statistics. The percentage of a country's population that lives in the cities serves is a benchmark for the success of the entire development process. It is reflects how well a country has dealt with the demanding forces of development and transformation. The more people a nation has living in cities, the greater the likelihood that more children will go to school and continue to go to school. Urban people are also more receptive to change and less bound by tradition. This means, for example, that large families become less important than they were in the rural scene, where additional children could be put to economic use in a farming society. Urban people are "wired"—that is, they are more outward looking in terms of world events and economic potential. The urban setting also provides career opportunities for women in a way that is usually not present in the countryside. Also, as the number (and the percentage) of women working—in the professions, in business, in retailing, and even in factories—expands, the inclination of young couples to have early and large families diminishes. A couple in their twenties with no children will see that they are able to live lives quite distinct from what they would be able to achieve in a rural setting with three or four children.

At the same time, in Taiwan, as in so many nations with high percentages of urban population and a relatively low RNI, there continues to be discussion over quality of life. It is not certain that fewer children, more leisure time, and a greater amount of consumer goods—the characteristics of young urban professional couples—necessarily mean a better life. These new scenarios are being demonstrated and learned about in the expanding cities of East Asia. Lifestyles are beginning to change, as are values. Young couples and their younger brothers and sisters are beginning to make decisions themselves about the sort of lifestyles they will seek. Such culture changes associated with these issues are of continuing interest to governmental planners and seniors as well.

Gross National Income

Finally, the ultimate index of a country's economic success and potential is captured by average per capita income. Here, we use Gross National Income in Purchasing Power Parity (GNI PPP). GNI PPP means that the question "How much do you earn an hour?" becomes "How many hours do you have to work to buy a new pair of shoes or a color television?" This index refers to Gross National Income converted to "international" dollars using a purchasing power parity conversion factor. International dollars indicate the amount of goods and services one could buy in the United States with a given amount of money, according to the Population Reference Bureau. In this case, the approximately $13,000 that is the adjusted GNI PPP for Taiwan gives you a clear comparison with, for example, China. The GNI PPP in China is $3,950—or approximately one-third that of Taiwan.

The combination of all of these demographic features of the Taiwan population presents you with a nation that has reaped the benefits of actively working to bring population growth into control. It shows the rewards of such efforts in the low rates of infant mortality, the high age of life expectancy; and the relatively prosperous per capita income earned by the Taiwan population.

POPULATION DISTRIBUTION

For the past four centuries the population distribution of Taiwan has been surprisingly constant. The great majority of the Taiwanese (early Chinese) population has lived on the western part of the island and mostly on the broad plains that lie between the mountain flanks and the waters of the Taiwan Strait. Villages, and later towns, have steadily migrated upslope, but the real centers of population were, and are, the cities that have harbors or highway and railway links with other urban centers on the north, west, and south sectors of the island. Few Chinese Taiwanese have moved to the highland area, and even fewer have gone upslope into the heights of the Chung Yang Shan.

ETHNICITY

Within the Taiwanese population there is a very strong Han Chinese ethnic imprint. One of the distinctive populations is the Hakka. Coming from North to South China in the 1200s, they are of Han Chinese origin. They have been clannish and are described as aloof as settlers of less fertile (but often less-contested) upslope landscapes. These lands, however, were much like the Guangdong hill lands they came from and this made their arrival and settlement less of a problem than it might otherwise have been.

The uplands traditionally have been home to the island's aboriginal tribes. Although indigenous peoples account for less than 2 percent of the total 22.5 million population, they have traditional presence and some governmental authority over the use of the forested lands that lie above the terraces and of the piedmont villages. These people—and there are (at least) ten different groups—have only slowly acculturated (mixed in) with the Taiwan Chinese. During the Japanese colonial period (1895–1945), they were a particularly resistant minority force and required considerable Japanese effort to bring them under control as the Japanese attempted to tap highland forest resources.

LANGUAGE AND RELIGION

When I taught at a Chinese university many years ago, I tried very hard to learn Chinese. I remember being very impressed with the man who ran the local "convenience store" near the place where we lived. Everyday he worked in four languages. He knew—and could use in his trade—Taiwanese, Mandarin Chinese, Japanese, and a few words of English. Such is the nature of trade in Taiwan, and the language patterns of the country reflect some of this.

The official language of Taiwan is Mandarin Chinese, even though Taiwan has many millions of Chinese who also speak Taiwanese, a variant of the Chinese Fujian dialect. There is still a smattering of Japanese spoken by the very senior people who were present during at least part of the Japanese colonial years. English has become an informal second language of urban Chinese, especially those employed (or wanting to be employed) in the dominant technology sector.

Finally, there are the aboriginal peoples with their distinctive languages. These minority peoples tend to be very poorly assimilated into urban society. Approximately one-third are of the Ami group. These people have maintained a reasonably strong presence in upland farming landscape of eastern Taiwan. They generally speak some Taiwanese and some Chinese as well as the Ami language.

RELIGION

Taiwan, like most islands of such size that lie on migration and shipping routes, is a product of influences from a wide variety of places. The aboriginal peoples, who began to migrate northward from Southeast Asia some 10,000 to 15,000 years ago, brought with them their own religious systems. Some still have expression in areas where the aborigines have been able to maintain some independence from the Chinese.

The Portuguese and Spanish introduced Roman Catholicism. The Dutch brought Protestant Christianity. On Taiwan today there are some 3,000 Protestant churches and 800 Catholic churches. The fact that these two branches of Christianity are so persistent today attests to the strong impact made by earlier Europeans and their religions.

The Japanese had a fifty-year tenure in Taiwan, and Shintoism is the major evidence of that colonial experience. It is, however, only slightly visible and, like other religions diffused (spread) to the island, its practices are generally intermixed with the dominant religious influences brought by the Chinese.

The people of Taiwan practice a variety of religions, from aboriginal faiths, to Roman Catholicism, to Confucianism. In this photograph men are dressed as Taoist gods during the annual Dragonboat festival in Taipei. This event is a traditional time to pray for the eradication of sickness and misfortune.

The Chinese contributed Buddhism and Taoism in their diffusion of religious belief systems from the mainland. There are some 3,000 Taoist and more than 2,000 Buddhist temples on the island. However, the really dominant so-called religion on Taiwan is Confucianism. Many will say that Confucianism is not a religion, but people who derive moral, ethical, and spiritual strength from Confucian beliefs and writings ascribe a very real religious importance to this system.

One of the most important things to note here is that Buddhism, Taoism, and Confucianism all are very accommodating as religions. That is, you may have small shrines to several of these belief systems in your house and such an overlap does not generally bother anyone. The Chinese have been frustrating to Western missionaries for centuries because of their capacity to openly accept Christianity, yet integrate it into their life system next to the icons of Taoism or Confucianism. The experience in Taiwan has been similar to that of the Chinese, except that the Taiwanese also have absorbed Japanese Shintoism in somewhat the same way.

The people of Taiwan are ethnically almost entirely Han Chinese, but they have come to the island from different times and different places. Their lifestyles have considerable variety and will be explored as we consider the essence of their government and economy since they are the institutions that give so much personality to this small parallel universe to mainland China.

CHAPTER

5

Political Geography

On the first page of Chapter 1 of this book, it was noted that Taiwan lies in the shadow of the massive People's Republic of China. While many other factors have had an impact on the history of Taiwan and its political geography, the crowning reality is that this is a small island that was once fully controlled by China. Even though it is now seeking to go in a different political direction, it still lies in the considerable shadow of the People's Republic.

Does this mean that no matter what else happens, no matter how productive the Taiwanese people are or how successful the government is, nearly everything is secondary in importance to the simple reality of location? The answer is, "Yes!" We will explore this concept in this chapter.

During recent decades, Taiwan has been very successful in the realms of economic development and involvement in global trade.

At the same time, the government has established an impressive record of reflecting the population's interest in democratic processes. The island has served as a model for other countries. It has successfully controlled population growth, it has captured market share in certain sectors of global trade, and it has made maximum use of its well-educated and highly skilled labor pools. However, the government has to return again and again to the reality that less than 100 miles (162 kilometers) to the west lies one of the largest countries in the world—a country that possesses the world's largest population. This country, China, says that Taiwan belongs to it and must return, in some form or other, to the Chinese collection of provinces, autonomous regions, and special municipalities. Taiwan is not eager for this to occur in any form.

A small country with a large population and booming economy has to be attentive to broader global conditions and opportunities on a daily basis. That is the nature of political life in Taiwan. From the island's political capital in the city of Taipei to the small factory owners who supply vital components to the island's economic output, most Taiwanese are aware that political activities in Taiwan are keenly tied to what decisions are made in Beijing, more than 1,000 miles (1,600 kilometers) distant. Before we explore this relationship in depth, it is useful to briefly recap Taiwan's political evolution through the four major eras of its history already discussed in the chapter on Historical Geography: the early colonial period; the Chinese pre-twentieth-century role; the Japanese colonial period; and the 1945–present era.

ERA I: THE EARLY COLONIAL PERIOD

As we have mentioned, the Portuguese, Dutch, and Spanish all made efforts to control Taiwan during the great era of European expansion during the sixteenth to nineteenth centuries. During this European Age of Discovery and Colonization, there were European ships sent around the globe, replete with missionaries, merchants, and pirates—virtually all of whom had increasing interest in capturing and controlling some of East Asia's riches. However, none were successful in the long run in occupying Taiwan. By 1661 the island was cleared of European colonial bases and almost all of the European merchants and foreign representatives had left, mostly for points south.

ERA II: THE CHINESE PRE-TWENTIETH-CENTURY ROLE

The Chinese Ming dynasty (1368–1644) had been a dominant force on most of mainland China—meaning the China that lay north, south, and west of the continental coast that stretched from the mouth of the Yellow (Huang) River and arched down to the mouth of the Pearl (Xi) River near the island of Hong Kong. But it had not been a major presence in the day-to-day lives of the farmers, fishermen, and villagers who lived on the east side of the low but troubling mountain ranges that defined the provinces of Zhejiang, Fujian, Guangdong (historically Che-chiang, Fukien, Kwangtung).

In the last decades of the seventeenth century, these coastal provinces of southeastern China experienced a serious famine. Farmers, with no government authorization, fled to Taiwan and began to expand the agricultural base established by earlier Chinese. By 1683 the island had fallen under Manchu rule (the new dynasty on mainland China) and the estimated 150,000 farmers who had left Fukien province were brought under the wing of control of the new Ch'ing (Qing) dynasty.

The new leaders of the Ch'ing dynasty began to see Taiwan as a potential threat to the stability of the mainland. The proximity of the island and the relative ease of crossing the Taiwan Strait—first to the Pescadores Islands and then on to the island itself—led some government officials to want to repatriate the tens of thousand Chinese who had not officially purchased land or did not have new families established on the island.

Other governmental leaders who had been involved in the effort to control Taiwan and secure useful ports and resource bases on the island were fully against abandoning the island. It was said that the financial trade in deerskins and sulfur alone

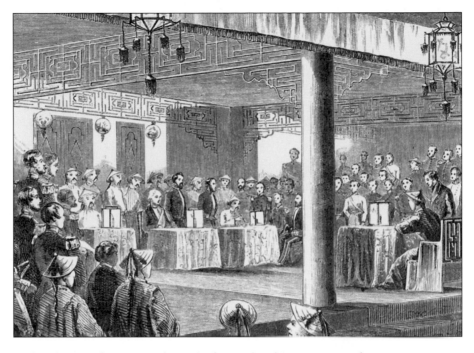

In the nineteenth century, the United States and Europe wanted access to Taiwanese ports to boost trade and give them access to opium. This struggle for port access led to the Opium Wars in 1839 and 1858. After its defeat in the second war, China signed the Treaty of Tien-ching with France, Britain, and the United States, seen in this illustration, which opened additional Chinese mainland ports to foreign trade.

was ample economic justification for holding on to the island. Additionally, it was claimed that if control of Taiwan was lost, the island would be left open to the continual threat of pirates (both Chinese and Japanese) who marauded the maritime trade in the East China Sea and Taiwan Strait.

Political forces desiring to continue the development of Taiwan ascended to power and, by 1842, it is estimated that some 2,500,000 people lived on the island. Rice, sugar, and some other economic resources were the elements of a steady trade between the western side of the island and the coastal provinces of the mainland.

With the Treaty of Tien-ching (signed by mainland China in 1858 with the British at the conclusion of what is sometimes called the Second Opium War), the Chinese were forced by the British to open some additional treaty ports. These ports—first created in 1842 with the British victory over the Chinese in the First Opium War (1839–1842)—were required to be open to foreign trade, particularly to the ever-growing population of Western mercantilists who wanted access to Chinese tea, silk, spices, art, and other exotics that had a grand market in European centers.

The two treaty ports opened in Taiwan after 1858 were Tainan in the south—the port that the Dutch had first settled two centuries earlier—and Tan-shui in the north. The Tan-shui port became the more significant commercial center, because it was close to the urban center of Taipei, which was growing into a major political center that soon became the focus of both foreign and domestic urban development.

In 1875 Taiwan became a full province, no longer just an annex to coastal China and Fukien Province. In 1895, Taipei became the official capital of the province. Some critics believe that the opening of Taiwan's ports to the outside world caused the "interiorization" of the island. The term describes the movement upslope and toward the interior of Taiwan by Chinese settlers who wanted to be free of any control by the Ch'ing government on the Chinese mainland. It is important to remember that much of this second era of Taiwan's development resulted from the migration of Chinese farmers who were trying to distance themselves from Chinese governmental control. For such people, the interior of Taiwan was more attractive than was the rapidly developing coastal zone.

ERA III: THE JAPANESE COLONIAL PERIOD

Japan's complete and devastating victory over the Chinese in the 1894–1895 Sino-Japanese War came as a shocking surprise to many observers. Japan was just two decades into its period of modernization that had begun with the Meiji Restoration in the late 1870s. Not even half a century had passed since American gunships had forced Japan to open its ports to the west. Traditionally, China had been the dominant cultural and political force in East Asia. The idea of the small island nation of Japan (smaller than the state of California) taking up arms against China—the traditional geographical and cultural giant of East Asia—was surprising enough, but to see the Japanese military so quickly dispatch the weak Ch'ing dynasty forces made many powers rethink their image of East Asia's military power at the close of the nineteenth century.

The Treaty of Shimonoseki, signed at the conclusion of the war, gave the island of Taiwan and its small islets lying to its west—the Pescadores—to Japan. For Japan, this was the country's first colonial experience. The success it had achieved allowed Japan to enter the twentieth century with a new level of confidence and ambition. Japan's control of Taiwan provided convincing evidence of the country's potential for playing a much more important role in the mercantile and military development of East Asia. Taiwan was seen as a rich resource, indeed.

In the 50 years that Japan held colonial control over Taiwan, there was great energy and investment capital spent in establishing a new infrastructure in the island. With the production of surplus rice and sugar as the two major targets for economic development, the Japanese invested capital in the elaboration of irrigation networks on the western side of the island. Additional capital was invested in the improvement of the surface transportation network between the north and southern parts of the island, particularly on the western plains, as well as in the education and militarization of the population.

With the establishment of a second Japanese colony, China's Manchuria, in the 1930s, Japan's military ambitions became more clearly evident in the region. In November 1943, toward the end of World War II, U.S. President Franklin D.

Roosevelt, British prime minister Winston Churchill, and China's Generalissimo Chiang Kai-shek met in Cairo, Egypt. The meeting was meant to signal continued full agreement of these three powers to fight against Japanese aggression. The resulting Cairo Agreement stipulated that Japan would have to submit to unconditional surrender and that all of its colonial holdings gained from 1895 on would have to be returned immediately.

To the Japanese, the potential loss of Taiwan would be particularly critical. The island had become a major staging ground for Japanese advances into Southeast Asia. Additionally, the island was seen by the Japanese as having the potential for serving as the geographic center of what the Japanese had defined as their "Greater East Asia Co-Prosperity Sphere," which was the Asian world the Japanese hoped to achieve upon completion of their military campaigns that had begun with the 1938 attack on China.

Nevertheless, the Japanese surrendered August 9, 1945 after the dropping of a second atomic bomb on the Japanese city of Nagasaki by United States forces. Taiwan and the Pescadores were returned to China by the end of October 1945. This transfer of power, like the one that had occurred 50 years earlier when China ceded Taiwan to Japan, took place without even the semblance of any effort to involve the Taiwan population. By late 1945, Chiang Kai-shek's Chinese Nationalists had begun their takeover of the political, military, and economic management of Taiwan. The Japanese Era had come to an end.

ERA IV: 1945–PRESENT

As Chiang Kai-shek's Nationalist (KMT) soldiers and their families began fleeing in huge numbers to Taiwan from the insurgent Communist forces of Mao Tse-tung (Mao Zedong) on the mainland, Taiwan felt that it was again losing its chance for independence. In the 1930s, a collection of local Taiwanese islanders had formed a group called the "Taiwan League for

Because of its proximity to mainland China, Taiwan has always felt it existed in the shadow of that country. This statue, standing over Taiwan's Matsu island group, of Chinese Nationalist General Chiang Kai-shek, who came to Taiwan in 1949 fleeing from Chinese Communists, is evidence of China's constant presence in Taiwan.

Local Self-Government." Author Steven Phillips points out that this group and this line of thought grew even stronger in Taiwan after the departure of the Japanese:

> Voicing themes that became common in disputes between the Nationalist state and the Taiwanese after 1945, indigenous political leaders emphasized that they were best able to manage the internal affairs of the island—they *should* have a greater role—and that their economic development and education levels warranted such measures—they *could* take on this responsibility. (Phillips in Rubenstein)

This frustration, based on a feeling that they were second-class citizens in what they considered to be their own island—or at least, in their own province—has plagued the Taiwanese increasingly for the past century. At first there was some toleration of the Chinese Nationalists in Taiwan. It was believed (in the 1940s and especially in the early 1950s) that the presence of the Chinese army and its leaders on the island was, in fact, a very temporary thing, to last only until they made their attack on the mainland's Communist armies. However, as time went on, such a return seemed ever more unlikely. The Chinese army's campaign in Tibet in 1950 gave the KMT some encouragement, because of the distraction distant Tibet seemed to provide to the Communist forces. At the same time, with North Korea's attack on South Korea in the summer of 1950, it appeared that China's military would soon be caught up in some "volunteer" involvement there as well, as reluctant allies of North Korea. Even though this did not happen, the Nationalists were still confident that they could launch an attack on the China coast and avoid major encounters with the Communists. From 1949—and the official victory of the Chairman Mao Tse-tung—Chiang Kai-shek's primary view of Taiwan was as a base for military preparations for the return to the mainland. It was never to be. When I taught in Taiwan in the early 1960s, I would see a Chinese colonel every morning on my dawn walk. He was dressed in full uniform and he would greet me with, "Today may be the day. THIS may be the day!" He meant, of course, that the call to begin the battle to reclaim the Chinese mainland might begin that very day. When I left Taiwan in 1964, he was still making that daily presentation of self in readiness for the increasingly mythic return.

The single most difficult event in the KMT assumption of full authority in Taiwan occurred in February 1947. Thomas Gold depicts it in this way:

Along with economic and political retrogression, the carpet-bagging Chinese brought lawlessness, corruption, plunder, inflation, disease, and an environment of general disorder. The Japanese physical and social infrastructure sustained a severe blow. Long quiescent, the Taiwanese penchant for violence exploded. On the evening of February 27, 1947, after Monopoly Bureau agents beat a woman selling cigarettes on the black market and shot a protesting bystander, a Taipei crowd attacked a police station, set fire to a police vehicle, and went on a rampage when the police refused to turn over the policemen who had fired the gun. . . . Figures for the total number of victims island-wide range from 10,000 to 20,000.

This uprising was without precedent in Taiwan. The Japanese had experienced occasional difficulties—especially with major policy and administration changes—but Taiwan's population had never taken to the streets this way. Although the "2/28 Incident" finally was partially settled, author Gold goes on to say:

> . . . the "2-28 Incident" . . . had a profound effect on the Taiwanese people. They had already seen the mainlanders plunder and wreck their economy and lower their material and cultural standard of living, which under the Japanese surpassed that of nearly all the rest of China.

One of the reactions to the 2/28 incident and the resulting carnage was an increasing reluctance of the Taiwan population to become involved in local politics. "Politics is dangerous" became a watchword for potential political leaders and local activists. As a result, there was very little volunteering for political work—especially if it was in opposition to the status quo—until well into the 1980s.

LAND TO THE TILLER PROGRAM

One of the most significant political innovations of the early era of Chinese Nationalist control of Taiwan came in the 1949–1953 "Land to the Tiller" program. In this nearly unprecedented agricultural reform program initiated by Ch'en Ch'eng, KMT governor of Taiwan, there were three dimensions:

1. Enforced rent reduction in farming.

2. Widespread sale of public agricultural lands.

3. Forced limit on the size of farm holdings.

The farm rent was reduced to a limit of 37.5 percent of the annual yield of the main crops on the rented farmland. The sale of public lands put approximately 180,000 *chia* (a *chia* is equal to about one hectare, or 2.5 acres, of land) of public land up for sale. This was nearly one-fifth of all the farmland on the island. The land was available for sale because the government had gained it from the Japanese holdings.

The limits for land ownership were set at 3 chia (7.5 acres) for medium-grade irrigated rice land and 6 chia (15 acres) for medium-grade nonirrigated land. Private holdings in excess of these limits were purchased by the government and then sold for small family farm operations. In this process some 350,000 acres (140,000 hectares) of farmland were transferred to 194,000 tenant farming families. This reduced the ratio of tenant farmers from 39 percent of the Taiwan agricultural population to 15 percent.

One immediate outcome of this program was a rapid increase in farm productivity and agricultural yields. The highest yields achieved during the Japanese colonial period were all surpassed by 1952. There was another payoff from this innovation: owners of the largest agricultural holdings—

who had been forced to sell much of the their land because their holdings exceeded the new limits—were paid for their land in industrial shares. This effected a shift from absentee landlordism to active role-playing in the island's new industrial programs.

Interestingly enough, this effort at land reform played out better than nearly any other similar effort in the world. In most revolutionary campaigns that seek to alter the farming world and its peasantry, there almost always remains a strong landowning group that is unwilling to allow its land to be divided up and given away to small farmers. subsequently there is often some modest change in land-holding arrangements, but the real task of getting land into the hands (and legal possession) of the small farmers is seldom achieved.

In Taiwan's "Land to the Tiller" program, the results were different because of the ownership situation facing the KMT government in the late 1940s and early 1950s. The social class that these new migrants from the Chinese mainland had most to fear was the population who had become wealthy under the Japanese colonial rule. By forcing these large landholders to sell (to the government) their excess land, the KMT greatly reduced the power base of this opposing economic and social group. It also made land available for the genuine tillers. Thus the program was very successful.

UNITED STATES – TAIWAN MILITARY CONNECTIONS

With the beginning of the Korean Police Conflict (the official name of the 1950–1953 Korean "War"), U.S. president Harry Truman ordered the U.S. Seventh Fleet to go to the Taiwan Strait. His intention was to show the Chinese Communists that the United States was taking sides—as it had during the prior decade in the Chinese Civil War—and was dedicating its force to the protection of the Chinese Nationalists. This bold naval move gave clear evidence of American support for Taiwan's political situation.

In 1951, the United States formalized and expanded its military and economic support of Taiwan with the establishment of the U.S. Military Assistance and Advisory Group. This group was based in Taiwan. In 1954, Taiwan and the United States signed the Mutual Defense Treaty. This treaty remained intact until 1971 when the United Nations recognized the mainland People's Republic of China (PRC) as the rightful holder of Taiwan's seat in this world body. The United States had worked diligently all through the 1950s and 1960s to slow down or thwart this critical political action, and it did not formally recognize mainland China until 1979, when the PRC became, officially, the sole legitimate authority in China.

TAIWAN'S CONNECTION TO THE PEOPLE'S REPUBLIC OF CHINA

Generalissimo Chiang Kai-shek died in 1975. His eldest son, Chiang Ching-kuo, assumed Taiwan's most powerful political role. However, since economic development was going so well and Taiwan's interaction with the broader world was steadily expanding in scope, Ching-kuo, beginning in 1986, allowed a more populist form of government to develop. For the first time since the KMT had arrived on the island and taken over the governing role, opposition political parties were allowed.

This change was given a major focus when the country's Taiwan-born vice president, Lee Tung-hui, was elected president in 1988 upon the death of Chiang Ching-kuo. Lee became the first president elected after a multi-party election campaign since the end of World War II. It also represented the first time that a Taiwan-born Chinese had been allowed to hold a major political position.

Lee Tung-hui was and is a central figure in the ongoing debate over the possible changing dynamic between China and the province of Taiwan. The Taiwan-born Chinese gained a Ph.D. in agricultural economics from Cornell University in

1968 and worked for 20 years for Taiwan's Joint Commission on Rural Reconstruction (JCRR). This gave him a perfect setting for bringing ideas of significant change to the sector of Taiwan's economy that most people assumed would be the major source of economic growth during the second half of the twentieth century.

From 1978 to 1981 Lee served as mayor of Taipei. After a productive term as mayor, Lee was appointed governor of Taiwan Province (1981–1984). In 1984 he was elevated to the position of vice president under Chiang Ching-kuo. With the subsequent death of Chiang in 1988, Lee became president.

In 1990, from June 28 to July 4, President Lee convened a National Affairs Conference in Taipei. This meeting occurred a year after the disastrous Tiananmen Square demonstrations in Beijing that had led to the deaths of many Chinese students who were rallying for more democratic freedoms. For Taiwan to convene such a conference—whose major themes of discussion were to center on aspects of democracy and student involvement in government—was a significant event. The conference covered five major issues:

1. Substantive parliamentary reforms, including agreement to hold an annual constitutional convention;

2. The nature of local governments on Taiwan, particularly a call for giving more authority to local decision makers;

3. The nature of central government, and its subordination to mainland China;

4. Whether the constitution needed to be revised, amended, or fundamentally rewritten;

5. Relations between Taiwan and mainland China.

The topic that generated the most heat was number 5, the issue of Taiwan's independence vs. reunification with the mainland. The political opposition to Lee Tung-hui (the Democratic Progressive Party, or the DPP) wanted Taiwan to come face to face with the necessity of deciding whether the island was going to promote reunification vs. independence. In 1990, Taiwan formally declared the end of its 40-year state of war with the People's Republic of China, but the issue was still not resolved.

The move toward greater independence from the mainland was accelerated by a 1991 decision by Taiwan's Council of Grand Justices (comparable to the U.S. Supreme Court) that required that all of the remaining Chinese mainlanders in Taiwan's National Assembly—those who had been elected to this post in 1948 on the mainland before the KMT lost the Civil War and fled to Taiwan—be retired within a year. These senior politicians had been, for nearly half a century, having discussions and making policy recommendations for the Chinese mainland, none of which ever were carried forth in China. This 1991 change further expressed Taiwan's wish to deal with the realities of the late twentieth century in East Asia. They gave up forever the idea of forcibly removing the Chinese Communists from power on the mainland.

In the following years of that decade, there was an erratic but steady effort to stabilize the relations between Taiwan (now called the Republic of China) and the mainland (the People's Republic of China). In an interview quoted in the *Encyclopedia Brittanica Book of the Year*, 1996, President Lee described Taiwan's attitude toward China in these words:

> Though Taiwan and the Chinese mainland are ruled separately by two autonomous political entities, most Chinese in the Taiwan area still maintain that the two sides should expand their international space individually while adhering to the premise of one China and that eventually reunification should be achieved by

gradually reducing the distance between the two sides and melding the two systems. Public opinion polls have repeatedly shown that advocates of independence for Taiwan have always been in the minority. Continued suppression of the ROC and deliberate obstruction of its international involvement by the mainland authorities will only feed this movement, however.

The following year, President Lee caused a major stir in these relations, because he went back to Cornell University—where he had received his doctoral degree—and attended a class reunion. Beijing saw this as the United States reneging on an agreement *not* to allow any major Taiwan executive official to visit the country. Lee argued that he went only as a graduate of the university. From this event came a decision by the PRC to fire long-range missiles into the waters north of Taiwan. These "tests" served as a reminder to the world that China still has the potential, the capacity, and the ultimate inclination to reclaim Taiwan as part of its country.

Late in 2003, tensions between the two Chinas got hot again as Taiwan's President Chen Shui-bian declared that in March 2004 elections, the Taiwan population would be able to demonstrate their inclinations toward the idea of independence from mainland China. This plan evoked great alarm in Beijing and even caused U.S. President George Bush to state that the United States would not support Taiwan's pursuit of full political independence from China.

This battle between the two Chinas continues to the present and, no doubt, will do so well into the future.

CHAPTER

6

Economic Geography

T hink of all the ideas that come into your mind when you hear the word economics. You might think of home economics, a subject your grandmother might have studied in high school. Perhaps economic development is a term you have learned in Social Studies as you looked at different examples of lifestyles in different countries. Economics may be a subject that is in your future if your high school has a required one-semester course in that subject. Or, maybe you just know it because you have heard your parents, teachers, and newscasters talking about the economy. In one way or another, it is a term that surrounds all of us.

Although geographers are keenly interested in a whole collection of factors—landforms, soil types, culture groups, migration patterns, climate—when they analyze places, their analyses return again and again to an area's level of economic development. Geographers want to know the important economic activities and the economic livelihood of the peoples being studied. What kinds of jobs people have—if they have jobs at all—and what economic opportunities they have is information that serves as the very foundation of geographic understanding of a country or a region—or even of a family. Economics is critically significant in understanding any locale, any place, and any human settlement.

THE TAIWAN MIRACLE

Thomas Gold wrote a book published in 1986 titled *State and Society in the Taiwan Miracle.* It is a study of the extraordinary economic progress the island made from the end of World War II to 1982. Consider these signs of economic growth that Gold outlines early in his book:

> GNP growth rates averaged 8.7 percent from 1953 to 1982, with a peak average of 10.8 percent for the years 1963–1972. The 1982 value of GNP was twelve times that of 1952. . . . The economy underwent a noticeable structural change as the contribution of industry outstripped agriculture and the leading sectors of industry changed as well, from processed food and textiles to electronics, machinery, and petrochemical intermediates. This indicates diversification and deepening of the economy. Trade surpluses occurred nearly every year since 1970. . . . Inflation was conquered, dropping from a murderous 3,000 percent in 1949 to 1.9 percent in the 1960s. . . . The gross savings rate has been above 20 percent of GNP every year since 1966 and more than 30 percent in ten of those years up through 1982. . . . The government showed budget surpluses every year from 1964 through 1981.

Table 3 puts some of these data into a simple format. This table shows the steady and generally impressive level of economic change in Taiwan in the three decades following the Korean War. During that period, the rate of population growth dropped more than 50 percent (from 3.8 percent to 1.8 percent), while

Table 3: Selected Years of Taiwan's Percentage Increase in Some Factors*

YEAR	POP. GROWTH	REAL GNP	GNP/ CAPITA	INDUSTRIAL PRODUCTION	EXPORTS	IMPORTS	INCOME/ CAPITA
1953	3.8	9.3	5.8	24.9	35.1	8.7	29.2
1959	3.9	7.7	4.3	1.8	47.8	50.2	11.2
1964	3.1	12.3	9.1	11.7	30.7	18.5	13.6
1970	2.4	11.3	9.0	9.0	41.2	25.7	12.6
1974	1.8	1.1	-0.7	-4.5	25.2	82.9	31.9
1980	1.9	6.6	4.6	9.3	22.9	33.5	22.0
1982	1.8	3.8	2.0	-1.7	4.2	-5.5	5.4

Source: Gold 1986, p. 6.

* These numbers represent the percentage increase from the prior year.

per capita income increased steadily. During much of the time, exports exceeded imports, allowing a positive trade balance. Taiwan's economic pattern has served as a model for many countries trying to make their economy work more productively and efficiently.

Another way to chart change is by noting that between 1963 and 1977, Taiwan's value of manufactured exports grew from $129,000,000 to $7,925,000,000. This means that this sector of manufactured goods was 61 times more productive in 1977 than it was in 1963. In East Asia, only South Korea was able to exceed that level of manufacturing growth.

Another index of change is GDP (gross domestic product),

Taiwan has made extraordinary economic progress from the end of World War II to the present day. Most notably, the economy has changed from being based in agriculture to being based in industries like electronics and machinery. This photograph shows Taiwanese executives and politicians preparing for the Computex Taipei technology exhibition, an important yearly event in Taiwan.

which, in Taiwan's case, shows that in 1960, 28 percent of Taiwan's GDP came from agriculture, whereas in 1978, only 10 percent came from agriculture. In that same period, the percent of GDP gained from industry grew from 29 percent to 48 percent. In 1978, Taiwan's life expectancy exceeded that of all East Asian countries except Hong Kong; both showed 72 years as their average life expectancy.

The data provided in Table 3 and Table 4 clearly show that Taiwan has made a profound economic change from its history of concentration on farm products. These changes are spotlighted in Table 4.

Table 4: Selected Indices of Taiwan's Growth

YEAR	POPU-LATION	RNI	AVERAGE FAMILY SIZE	LIFE EXPECT-ANCY	$GNP	EXPORTS GOODS AS % OF FOREIGN TRADE	IMPORTS GOODS AS % OF FOREIGN TRADE
1987	19.3 mil	1.3	4.5	F: 73 M: 70	$60 bil	11% electronics; 10% garments; 6% plastics	17% petroleum; 5% grains; 3% iron and steel
1990	19.9 mil	1.2	4.2	F: 76 M: 71	$119 bil	11.6% electronics 8% plastics; 6% garments	8% elec. products; 5% petroleum; 2% iron and steel
1993	20.6 mil	1.0	4.0	F: 77 M: 71	$180 bil	6% data processing equip.; 4% garments; 4% radio, electronics	30% machinery; 11% chemicals; 8% iron and steel
1995	20.9 mil	1.0	3.9	F: 77 M: 72	$220 bil	20% nonelectric machinery; 19% elec. mach; 6% plastics	18% elec. mach; 13% nonelec. mach; 9% iron and steel
1999	21.4 mil	.8	3.6	F: 78 M: 72	$297 bil	24% nonelec. mach.; 22% elec. mach.; 21% plastics	16% elec. mach.; 11% nonelec. mach.; 11% chemicals
2001	21.9	.7	3.4	F: 79 M: 73	$298 bil	50% machinery, elec.; 13% textiles; 6% plastics	17% elec. machinery; 12% nonelec. mach. 10%; chemicals
2003	22.5	.6	3.3	F: 79 M: 74	$288 bil	67% mach. and elec.; 12% textiles; 7% plastics	25% elec. mach.; 16% nonelec. mach.; 13% minerals

Source: *Encyclopedia Britannica Book of the Year*, various years. (Note: Dates in book reflect data from one or sometimes two years earlier.)

Table 4 gives you a window through which to view major economic changes that have occurred in Taiwan over the past two decades. Consider these facts that are contained in the data in this table:

- The rate of natural population increase (RNI) decreased from 1.3 percent in 1987 to 0.6 percent in 2003. This means that capital invested in economic growth and development during those decades was more available for factory development and industrial infrastructure.

- Average family size on the island decreased from 4.5 people in 1987 to 3.3 people in 2003. This has social implications as well as economic significance. Couples having only one or two children generally have more income to spend on goods, services, shelter, and leisure activities. All of these alternatives help stimulate the economy.

- Changes in life expectancy generally reflect greater availability of medical care, better nutrition, and probably a higher degree of urban residence in the overall population. For Taiwan, these have all occurred. The life expectancy levels now are among the highest in East Asia.

- The Gross National Product has increased nearly fivefold from 1987 to 2003. As we discussed earlier, Taiwan's 22.5 million people produce an economic output that is more than one-fifth that of mainland China—a nation with a population of 1.3 billion! Both the rapid increase in Taiwan's economic base and the overall magnitude of the island's economic productivity provide the country's economic

Even though its political identity is often in question, Taiwan is now a country of economic and international significance. Taiwan recently gained attention in 2003 for the completion of the world's tallest building, a one hundred and one-story tower in Taipei known as Taipei 101.

planners and entrepreneurs a strong sense of accomplishment. Such progress makes the island a role model for other small countries trying to change from a fundamentally agricultural to a more industrial economy. In the eyes of Taiwan's planners, the island's change is now going beyond greater industrialization and is heading toward the financial and intellectual service industries, in the mode of a postindustrial country.

- The patterns of imports and exports show the major transformation toward the export of machinery (both electrical and nonelectrical), electronics goods, and plastics. Textiles continue to play a minor role because they utilize the high-technology machinery and chemical imports for the creation of synthetic fabrics and clothes.

The overall picture of economic growth and change in Taiwan demonstrates that, regardless of its political status, the country must be seen as a contemporary economic power of major significance.

7

Taiwan's Regional Identities

A geographer is concerned with the way places look. What gives a location an identity? Why, for example, does the term "Big Sky Country" (the western-U.S. world of mountains and plains) so often evoke interest? Why does the name of Paris, France, have such imagery? The answers to these questions relate to the built environment, the physical setting, and the way in which humans have used and described such places. They all have a regional identity.

The three images that follow will help provide a sense of Taiwan's regional appearance—of what its geography has done to create a strong identity in the mind of Taiwanese and travelers who have been drawn to the island. Each description provides a set of geographical images that can help you to see Taiwan from afar.

THE CITY SCENE AND URBAN WIND SURFERS

The first set of images comes from the *Asian Wall Street Journal*

Weekly and is written by a journalist who has degrees in both geography and journalism. She is writing about a Pacific Ocean cove that lies due east of the urban center of Taipei, the capital of Taiwan. The cove is located on the island's thinly settled northeastern coast, about 30 miles (50 kilometers) from Taipei.

FULUNG WINDSURFING, NORTHEAST COAST DRIVE CAN BLOW AWAY CITY HASSLES

By J.R. Wu

TAIPEI—From the confines of cubicles and surrounded by the concrete metropolis of Taipei or Hsinchu, former students of Peter Zhi-hong Chan often call him in the middle of the day to ask, "What's the wind like?"

Off the shores of Fulung on the northeast coast of Taiwan, the waves ripple lightly in the shallow inlet that is the mouth of the Shuangshi River and pound more strongly on the other side of the sandbank that divides it from the mighty Pacific Ocean, making this area a prime spot for windsurfing for both beginners and experts.

Many weekend surfers and beach bums leave their mopeds and cars and the anarchy of urban traffic at home, paying NT$62–NT$132 (US$1.77–US$3.77) for a one-way ticket to the wind. The one-hour train ride from Taipei transports water worshippers to Fulung, where the train station itself is a two-minute walk from the beach.

I signed up for the three-day windsurfing course that cost NT$4,800 (US$137) and is run by Fulung Sail Service System, which was set up as the first sailing club in Taiwan in 1978— incidentally, on a typhoon day—and which survives as one of the dwindling number of sports clubs around the island.

My class of three began its windsurfing career at the changing of the winds that usually occurs after the Dragon Boat Festival around May–June each year when winter's northeasterly gives way to summer's southwesterly.

We faced force winds of between four to seven, which measures about 11 to 30 knots, during our first two days of instruction. For beginners like myself and my two classmates—both unrelated, but named Mr. Chang, and who both discovered windsurfing when on holiday in Sabah, Malaysia—force winds of three and under make the best conditions for learning the basics of board balance, uphauling the sail, gripping and maneuvering the boom and, finally, surfing on the water with the wind at our backs.

Dozens of boards and rolled-up sails stuffed in cubbyholes, catamarans, Optimist and Laser dinghies, a colorful array of sailing outfits and a lineup of trophies won by club members make up the decor in the warehouse facilities, which are located right on Fulung Beach and adjacent to the Lungmen camping grounds.

Though this island boasts 898 miles of both sandy and rocky coastline, windsurfing remains a relatively undeveloped sport in Taiwan, explains Mr. Chan, as he stands in the classroom that faces the Pacific and demonstrates the basic theory of knot-tying, gybing [altering the course through 180 degreees] and tacking on a white erasable-ink board and a model-size wind-surf board he had made from a piece of carved wood (the board), part of a fishing pole (the mast), a hanger wire (the boom) and goggle straps (the footstraps).

Windsurfers here for the most part carry their cellphones in a small waterproof pouch, which is a means for them to call to shore for help if necessary as regulations for rescue and survival in leisure and sport sailing remain under the domain of commercial fishing in Taiwan.

Technology's convenience means windsurfers mostly dial ashore to report, "The wind here is bei bai!"—in other words, not bad at all, says Mr. Chan, adding that it remains up to him and members of the family-like club to stay alert and regularly scan the waters to account for every windsurfer.

Unfortunately, Mr. Chan also notes, the absence of watersport regulations also means jetskiers and motorized waterbikes rev through the same waters around the inlet, leaving behind exhaust and a choppy wake.

The club has a license to sail the 10,559 acres of waters enclosed in the natural bay between the capes of Santiaochiao to the south and Pitouchiao to the north.

Lush, steep mountains and hills on one side and rocky shorelines revealing stark, sea-eroded tablelands on the other flank the curvy lanes of Route 2 that run along this area known as the Northeast Coast National Scenic Area, which seems to be a sister coastline to California's Highway 1.

From the lighthouse on the tip of Santiaochiao, which is Taiwan's easternmost point, the Spanish soldier Santiago who landed in 1626 likely glimpsed Kueishan Island, named after the shape of a turtle.

Taiwan's northeast coast is also a prime area for Chinese fishermen barely eking out a bitter living at sea to smuggle ashore and participate in the newly industrialized economy that is Taiwan. The ban on direct cross-strait travel [between Taiwan and mainland China] has in part kept leisure sailing from developing in earnest in Taiwan out of fear sportive sailors may attempt to cross the Taiwan Strait, which separates Taiwan and mainland China by about 93 miles.

Some of the earliest settlers in the administrative unit of Gungliao Village, which includes Fulung and the small towns nestled along the shores of the northeast coast between Lungtung and Santiaochiao, came from China's Fujian province, including Wu Sha, who settled in the area in the late 1700s and is considered an ancestor to many in the village.

North of Lungtung where nine-hole [sea] shells are harvested and just west of the nose-shaped cape of Pitouchiao, the waters near the old gold-mining towns of Jinkuashih and Chiufen are sometimes called the "yin-yang sea" because of the two-toned gold and blue hue that sometimes appears as the ocean meets the silt near the shoreline.

As I pound away in front of my computer screen to meet deadlines in my air-conditioned office while outside nondescript buildings crowding the capital bake in the windless summer heat, I'm tempted to call Mr. Chan to ask, "What's the wind like?"

The images that should capture your imagination in this newspaper essay must include the contrast between the city of Taipei (pop. 2.6 million) and the island's thinly settled northeast coast. There is the image, too, of the small pouch with the cell phone. The city dweller can chance his or her luck with wind and waves, but still stay in close touch with office mates or friends who are in the city wondering "What's the wind like?"

In Taiwan, as in most of the world, part of a location's identity is created by the variety of landscapes you associate with it. In Taiwan and Taipei, this close bond with ocean windsurfing is a part of this region's identity.

A FARMING SCENE

On the flanks of Big Belly Mountain (Tatu Shan) on the western outskirts of Taichung in west-central Taiwan, one can find many traditional rural landscapes. In the past, the closer to the coast these farmlands lay, the more likely they were to be given over to irrigated rice beds. Now the lands nearer the edge of the coastal plain are more likely to be transformed into expanding urban settings, as has much of the prime farmland on the island during the rapid Taiwan urbanization of the past three decades.

But, as you go upland, more traditional farmland can be seen. The images of this setting come from the patterns a few miles from the campus of Tunghai University, outside the ever-expanding margins of the city of Taichung. Traditional farming homes built of mud blocks sit atop foundations of rock often gathered from local streambeds. These water-rounded shapes are mortared together. Homes of prosperous families are built around an interior courtyard; there is most often a tamped earth or concrete surface in front of the major door. In these households, sons got married and brought their wives to live in the traditional farmstead. Children and grandchildren were born. The rural extended family was the influence that caused these farmsteads to add space and family complexity. This still continues, even in rapidly urbanizing Taiwan. However, such a pattern is most likely to continue in rural farming areas more distant from major cities.

As these farm families grew, additional rooms were added to the sides of existing structures, creating an intricate net-work of courtyard, passageways, and rooms of varying size and importance. Some homes have a stone or adobe wall built around them; others remain unenclosed, thereby making it easier to bring rice and other crops to this sunlit and hard surface for processing. On the dry surface, the grain is warmed, raked, left in the sun, raked again, and slowly prepared for the critical task of husking—the removal of the husks that cover each grain of brown rice.

Some of the traditional farmsteads also had animal pens off to the side or at the back of the house. Older farmers in Taiwan will still talk of how animals used to occupy the bottom floor while the family lived and slept upstairs. Traditional farmers—men and women in their 60s and 70s—recall the way in which the farm fields used to come right up to the foundations of the

The crowded streets of Taiwan's cities are a stark contrast to the rural landscapes in some areas of Taiwan. Though the rapid industrialization of recent decades has threatened the lifestyle of Taiwanese farmers, many families still operate traditional farms. This photograph shows farmers drying rice on the banks of the Peikong River.

structures and to the edges of the rice grain drying pad. The need to use every square foot of productive land for crops produced the classic pattern of Chinese farmlands. In China and Taiwan, land is farmed more intensively than almost anywhere else in the world.

Not only are homes now more often built of brick and stone, but many are now two stories high. New farm families now take over all of the ground-level space. In addition, the mud blocks that were so important in farm buildings as recently as the 1960s are now being razed and replaced by new farm structures made of stone, brick, or wood.

Rather than being farmed, land next to the home and farm buildings now may be used for other purposes. Space for parking cars has become important. Gardens—which have always been a significant use of the most fertile land right near the kitchen of the farmstead—continue to have their special locations, but now there is some land given over to flowers in place of or in addition to vegetables.

Older farmers here also have another powerfully changed dimension to their lives. While they still work the land—and irrigated rice is still the most important crop—these seniors speak of the distinctive future to be enjoyed by their children and grandchildren who have gone to college (some even to nearby Tunghai University). In the past, few rural youngsters were able to gain access to college. But in modern Taiwan, this doorway is now open. There is near-complete compliance with Taiwan's laws requiring primary schooling, and it is becoming increasingly common for youngsters to stay in school as long as they are able to pass the higher level exams that grant them access to still more education. Even to Chinese farm children, it has been made clear that education is the route that can lead to a career free from the very demanding labors of farming.

Many successful students go to the United States for graduate school and then return to Taiwan for careers in engineering, marketing, computer science, or education. The historical "brain drain" (when the brightest children of a Lesser Developed Country [LDC] go abroad for college and graduate education and remain to work in that newly adopted country) has been declining. Many if not most international graduates return to Taiwan and its booming economy. This phenomenon, then, yields a polarized socioeconomic landscape: suburban housing developments and networks of new and expanded highway systems increasingly surround traditional farmland. Youngsters are educated and work in urban environments as professionals, yet their grandparents continue to live in traditional ways and continue to work as farmers.

However, the land ownership situation is somewhat unique. Because of the increasing value of their land, many farmers are, in fact, land-wealthy. They know that their land, close to Taichung (pop. over 1 million), is extremely valuable and can be sold at an enormous profit compared to what they paid for it when they took title under, for example, the Land to the Tiller program in the 1950s.

TAROKO GORGE

This regional hallmark of the natural beauty of Taiwan lies on the eastern side of the island. Taroko Gorge is a canyon that lies just north of Hualien, the city at the northern end of the long rift valley that separates the Central Mountains from the Coastal Mountain Range. It is a part of the landscape of Taiwan that was largely left to some of the aboriginal groups who peopled Taiwan prior to the arrival of the Han Chinese.

Aboriginal peoples found the mountain setting relatively attractive because of the isolation it afforded them from the Chinese. The Central Mountain Range formed a barrier between them and the steadily growing populations of the western mountain flank. The mountains of the Taroko Gorge on the eastern side of the island also provided abundant fresh water, a modest amount of land that could accommodate shifting cultivation, and adequate space for village settlement.

In the 1950s, however, things in this ten-mile gorge began to change in a major way. The Japanese, between 1895 and 1945, had given some minor attention to the development of hot springs facilities on the eastern side of Taiwan. During this time Taroko underwent some development, but it wasn't until a half-century ago that the Taiwan government began a major effort to better link the well-settled western part of the island with the pristine lands of the eastern rift valley and coastline. Thus, the Taroko Gorge became a link in the new Central Cross-Island Highway.

The road was begun in 1956. In 1960, it was opened to commercial traffic. Some 450 workers died during its construction from the hazards associated with cutting a roadway through cliff faces that were hundreds of feet high. The road also had an early history of being buffeted by typhoons, closed by rock slides, and often, during construction, open only in one direction or another because there was so little working space for machinery.

In addition to the challenges inherent in building an all-season road—much of it cut through rock faces—another problem emerged. Marble was discovered during the road construction process. Taiwan then went through a spurt of exporting handsomely crafted marble statuary, building block, and even dinnerware. As a result, there was a minor effort by some to close the gorge to traffic and mine the whole area. That position did not prevail, but there is still a residual marble operation in the gorge.

The real benefit of this major enhancement to the regional environment was the role tourism began to play. Today, Taroko Gorge is the island's second-ranking tourist destination— after Taipei and its urban excitement. As an aspect of regional identity, the gorge represents the strong environmental variety that the island presents to, particularly, prosperous Japanese and other East Asian tourists who find the range of urban and natural delights in this small island worthy of the expenditure of considerable tourist capital.

Regional identity in Taiwan is shaped by both physical features and cultural patterns. The merging of villages near cities into suburbs of those cities is modifying traditional identities all up and down the west coast of the island. The transformation of urban areas from local urban centers to regional capitals of finance and commerce characterized by

Taroko Gorge, the hallmark of natural beauty seen in this photograph, is a ten-mile canyon in eastern Taiwan. After the construction of the Central Cross-Island Highway through the gorge in 1960, the gorge became Taiwan's second most popular tourist destination, representing the environmental variety of the country.

industrial innovation and managerial expertise has spread the forces of change across Taiwan's urban shores. Farmers, in some cases, have become real estate developers. Children of farmers often become dentists and electrical engineers. Women whose mothers had only modest options beyond village life and the mothering of families of four or five children are now playing roles in the management of computer engineering and software development firms.

Taiwan continues to be an island of change. Its regional identities are fluid and increasingly associated more with the totality of East Asian development and less with the specifics of Taiwan tradition.

8

Taiwan's Future

At the outset of this book, it was suggested that Taiwan could be seen as a parallel universe to the historical drama and economic power of the People's Republic of China. This allusion was made because of the existence of similar patterns of economic change, population management, and—to a much lesser degree—political significance on both sides of the Taiwan Strait. As mentioned, the island of Taiwan has an area equal to less than 1 percent of that of the Chinese mainland, and the island's population of 22.5 million is not even 2 percent of China's. Yet, in terms of how the present will shape the future, Taiwan is destined to play a major role in the future development of East Asia. Three dimensions of Taiwan will shape the future of the island, and of the region:

1. Taiwan's political link with the People's Republic of China;

2. The island's capacity to continue major economic growth; and

3. Its ability to continue democratic development.

LINK WITH THE PRC

The political connection with the People's Republic is at the heart of the future for Taiwan. Objective analysis points out that Taiwan is seen by the PRC as a renegade Chinese province that, as such, will have to be reunited with the mainland. The example of South and North Korea—divided after the end of World War II because of political tensions between their governments in Seoul (South Korea) and Pyongyang (North Korea)—looms large in the minds of all who ponder the future for Taiwan.

On Taiwan, the most vocal forces seek full political independence for the island, yet they know that there is profound danger in explicit declaration of a governmental intention to become a fully independent nation. There has been much talk of such a move during political campaigns, but once the victor—such as the current president Chen Shui-bian—wears the full mantle of authority, it seems much more difficult to continue movement toward such a scenario. China is very close, China is very large, China is very strong—and China is very certain it does not want to give up Taiwan.

The difficulty with the other viewpoint—the belief that there will be some sort of reunification of Taiwan and the PRC—is that even with the mainland making extraordinary gains in economic growth, there seem to be few potential benefits, in the eyes of most Taiwanese, to being part of such a massive and authoritarian regime. The only clear benefit, it is felt, would be resolution of the problem of Taiwan's possible flight into complete political independence. It is often pointed out by the PRC that reunification would enable a much more open and efficient flow of goods, people, and technology between the two Chinas.

Thus this first issue—dealing with political autonomy for Taiwan—is the giant one, paramount over all others. Taiwan's future will be shaped most completely by the resolution of this tension. It is an anxiety felt by Chinese on both sides of the Taiwan Strait.

CONTINUING MAJOR ECONOMIC GROWTH

As these final pages are being written, the *Wall Street Journal* has published an article indicating that Taiwan now has the third highest number of cases of the often deadly severe acute respiratory syndrome (SARS). This fact is one of those world rankings that no one ever wants to achieve. For several years, Taiwan has maintained a dominant role in the production of notebook computers (number 1 in world production), desktop computers, and peripherals (among the top three in the world). This high level of productivity is difficult to reverse, yet SARS has become a source of confusion, alarm, and declining productivity that was never anticipated. In both government and private industry, planning energies are primarily focused upon aspects of economic competition, technological innovation, and global marketing strategies. Unexpected health crises are seldom factored into development scenarios. As *Wall Street Journal* reporters Jason Dean and Karen Richardson point out:

> The mounting toll and the spread of SARS from Taipei to other parts of the island is fueling concern about the economic costs of the disease. Wu Rong-i, president of the Taiwan Institute of Economic Research, said his think tank projected a few weeks ago that if SARS is brought under control by late June [2003], economic growth in 2003 would slow to 3% from its earlier forecast of 3.5%. "But, if it becomes worse and continues after June, as it seems possible now, then we should consider something more severe," he said, adding that full-year growth could be as slow as 1.8%.

Taiwan's future depends on many factors, including its connection with the People's Republic of China, its democratic development, and its economic progress. If Taiwan can sustain the growth it had during recent decades, it should continue to play a major role in East Asia and the world. The view of Taipei at night in the photograph is similar to the view in any of Taiwan's bustling, modern metropolitan areas.

Taiwan's planners and capitalists were able to raise the per capita GNP from $1,100 in the early 1950s to nearly $14,000 during the early years of the twenty-first century. This huge increase illustrates what a powerful economic engine Taiwan has developed. Because of this achievement, Taiwan has become one of Asia's newly prosperous "Four Tigers" (along with Hong Kong, Singapore, and South Korea). The challenge that the island now faces is to rebound from the SARS problem and stay fully competitive with the other Asian Tigers and the Dragons—China, Malaysia, Indonesia, and the Philippines—which together are labeled the Newly Industrializing Economy

(NIE), shorthand for the most aggressive economies of the East Asian region.

Judging from the enviable record that Taiwan has established during the past quarter-century, it appears that the island will be quite efficient in staying toward the front of the pack in such global efforts as economic innovation and marketing.

ABILITY TO CONTINUE DEMOCRATIC DEVELOPMENT

One of the factors in Taiwan's very rapid pace of economic development in the past 25–30 years has been the reversal of the so-called brain drain. In the early 1960s, there began a rush of bright Chinese students from Taiwan to American and British universities for undergraduate and graduate study. Taiwan sent many of its brightest students to foreign schools in the hope that they would then find a returning population of well-trained professionals who would help guide the island toward stable economic growth and change.

Too often, however, students found that they were offered solid academic and professional positions in Western universities or companies upon their completion or near completion of their college degree programs. For the overseas Chinese student, the idea of accepting a university position or research role in an active and well-supported Western think tank proved to be very attractive. In the 1960s, when Taiwan and China were bound up in political tension and Taiwan had not yet begun its rapid development of industrial markets and exports, the equation seemed stacked in favor of students staying in the United States or Europe.

Beginning in the mid-1980s, however, many more Taiwanese students began to return home upon completion of their studies abroad. It was, in fact, these human resources that Taiwan began to use so effectively, such as in the development in 1980 of Hsinchu Science Park in northwest Taiwan and a similar facility near Tainan built a decade later.

Since 1996 when the Taiwan people elected their first president, democratic institutions have continued to gain strength, while the Kuomintang has lost power. In this photograph, Nationalist Party chairman Lien Chan and People First Party chairman James Soong unveil their logo for the 2004 presidential campaign.

In the early years of the twenty-first century, brain drain once again began to pose a problem but with a new spin. Well-educated Taiwan Chinese began to be courted by ambitious and well-funded firms on the Chinese mainland. To the mainland operators, employing such "immigrants" as those from Taiwan meant obtaining well-trained employees with full language abilities (Chinese and often English as well). This hiring effort also began to soften the rough edges that existed between Taiwan and the PRC. The downside of this pattern of immigration for the mainland Chinese was that the Taiwan Chinese had been exposed to democratic institutions at their Western universities, thus posing the potential for at least minor political disruption in the PRC.

Over one-fifth of Taiwan's population is under fifteen. The country's government has been very attentive to dealing with this sector of the population by developing educational institutions and tending to individual needs. The government believes social well-being and economic success depends on accommodating the needs of the young, such as these children who are visiting the Chiang Kai-Shek memorial.

Within the past decade particularly, there has been a steady expansion of democratic institutions on Taiwan. The political landscape began to include not one but several political parties. As mentioned earlier, in 1996 the Taiwan people themselves elected their first president (Lee Tung-hui). The Kuomintang (KMT) Party continues to exist, but it is steadily losing political clout. The Democratic Progressive Party (DPP) has been the ascendant party, but it was the New Party (NP) that supported and helped elect current president Chen Shui-bian in 2000. That election ended a half-century of KMT dominance in the political scene in Taiwan.

CONCLUSION

As noted a number of times, there are many social, demographic, and economic factors in Taiwan that seem to be microcosms of those in the People's Republic of China. Taiwan is, in so many ways, a parallel universe to the largest nation on earth. However, the one factor that separates these two political entities is the very distinct and different political character of each of the two Chinas. As the future plays out, this distinction will serve as a dominant force in demonstrating whether or not Taiwan is a truly parallel universe.

Fact at a Glance

Land and People

Full Country Name Republic of China

Area 13,969 square miles (35,980 square kilometers)

Highest Point Yu Shan (13,114 feet; 3,997 meters)

Population 22,500,000

People Taiwanese (including Hakka), 84%; mainland Chinese, 14%; aborigine, 2%.

Urban Population 77%

Life Expectancy 77 years

Capital Taipei

Major Cities Taipei, Kaohsiung, Taichung, Tainan, Keelung

Official Language Mandarin Chinese

Other Language Taiwanese

Religions Buddhism, 24%; Taoism, 21%; I-kuan Tao, 4%; Protestant, 2%; Catholic, 1%.

Economy

Major Products Electronics, chemicals, plastics, textiles, iron and steel, food

Gross National Product $314.4 billion (2001)

Economic Sectors Electronics, iron and steel, machines, textiles, plastics, agriculture

Currency New Taiwan dollar (NT); 34 NT = US$1.00

Average Annual Income $14,220 (2000)

Government

Form of Government	Multiparty democracy with 5 branches (Legislative Yuan, National Assembly; Executive Yuan; Judicial Yuan; Examination Yuan; Control Yuan)
Head of State	President
Head of Government	Prime Minister
Voting Rights	Universal suffrage at age 20
Political Divisions	Provinces (hsien), cities (shih)

History at a Glance

800	Chinese known to have records of the island, but little interest in it.
1590	Portuguese discover Taiwan, name it "Ilha Formosa" (Beautiful Island).
1622	Dutch introduce Protestant religion to Taiwan.
1624	Spanish introduce Roman Catholic religion to Taiwan.
1624	Dutch settle Anping in southwestern Taiwan.
1626	Spanish settle Keelung in northeastern Taiwan.
1661	Chinese warrior Cheng Ch'eng-kung (Koxinga) expels Dutch, Spanish.
1683	Taiwan falls to Manchu (Ch'ing Dynasty) control, the new dynasty on the Chinese mainland.
1858	Tainan port in southwest Taiwan and Tamshui in northwest Taiwan named Treaty Ports as part of continuing British-Chinese response to Opium War.
1895	Treaty of Shimonoseki between China and Japan gives Taiwan to the Japanese, who control the island until the end of World War II in 1945.
1943	Cairo Agreement turns Taiwan over to Chinese Nationalists at the end of World War II (October 25, 1945).
1949–1950	Some 1.8–2.0 million Nationalist Chinese leave the mainland for Taiwan.
1949	Taiwan begins "Land to the Tiller" program.
1950	U.S. President Truman puts U.S. Seventh Fleet in Taiwan Strait to thwart possible military effort from the Communist Chinese to take over the island.
1954	Taiwan and United States sign Mutual Defense Treaty on December 2.
1971	People's Republic of China (PRC) replaces Taiwan in the United Nations.
1979	United States establishes diplomatic relations with PRC.

1986 KMT allows opposition parties in Taiwan politics.

1988 Travel restrictions to mainland China are eased but trade goods from Taiwan still go through Hong Kong rather than directly to China.

1995 KMT role is sharply reduced in Taiwan island politics and President Lee Tung-hui returns to alma mater Cornell University for a class reunion. China fires missiles into waters north of Taiwan in response.

1996 For the first time, Taiwan's president (Lee Tung-hui) is directly elected from the population.

1997 Taiwan holds a 70,000-person antireunification protest in Taipei as control of Hong Kong is returned to the People's Republic of China in July.

2000 President Chen Shui-bian is first president with no connection to Kuomintang Party ever to be elected.

2000 Taiwan's application to join the World Trade Organization is approved.

2003 Taiwan develops significant number of SARS cases; tourist trade falls significantly as it does also in China.

Bibliography

Dean, Jason, and Karen Richardson. "Impact of SARS on Taiwan Casts Economic Cloud." *Asian Wall Street Journal.* May 23, 2003.

Doing Business in Taiwan. New York: Price Waterhouse, 1996.

Gold, Thomas B. *State and Society in the Taiwan Miracle.* Armonk, New York: M.E. Sharpe, Inc., 1986.

Knapp, Ronald G. *China's Old Dwellings.* Honolulu: University of Hawaii Press, 2000.

Knapp, Ronald G. "The Shaping of Taiwan's Landscapes." In *Taiwan: A New History.* Ed. Murray A. Rubinstein. New York: M.E. Sharpe. 3–26, 1999.

Kolb, Albert. *East Asia: Geography of a Cultural Region.* Suffolk, Great Britain: Methuen & Co., 1971.

Lamley, Harry. J. "Taiwan under Japanese Rule, 1895–1945." In *Taiwan: A New History.* Ed. Murray A.Rubenstein. New York: M.E. Sharpe. 201–260, 1999.

Phillips, Steven. "Between Assimilation and Independence: Taiwanese Political Aspirations under Nationalist Chinese Rule, 1945–1948." In *Taiwan: A New History.* Ed. Murray A. Rubenstein. New York: M.E. Sharpe. 275–319, 1999.

Reischauer, Edwin O., and John K. Fairbank. *East Asia: The Great Tradition.* Boston: Houghton Mifflin Company, 1960.

Rubenstein, Murray A., ed. *Taiwan: A New History.* New York: M.E. Sharpe, 1999.

Storey, Robert. Melbourne and Oakland, Calif.: Lonely Planet Publications, 2001.

Wang, Peter Chen-main. "A Bastion Created, a Regime Reformed, an Economy Reengineered, 1949–1970." In *Taiwan: A New History.* Ed. Murray A. Rubenstein. New York: M.E. Sharpe. 320–338, 1999.

Bates, Christopher. *Culture Shock! Taiwan: A Guide to Customs and Etiquette*. Portland, OR: Graphic Arts Center Publishing Company, 2003.

Fowler, Beth. *Half Baked in Taiwan*. New York: XLibris (Random House) Publishing, 2000.

Gold, Thomas B. *State and Society in the Taiwan Miracle*. Armonk, New York: M.E. Sharpe, Inc., 1986.

Haw, Stephen G. *A Traveller's History of China*. New York: Interlink Books, 2001.

Huntington, Madge. *A Traveler's Guide to Chinese History*. New York: Henry Holt and Company, 1986.

Knapp, Ronald G. *China's Old Dwellings*. Honolulu: University of Hawaii Press, 2000.

Roy, Denny. *Taiwan: A Political History*. Ithaca, NY: Cornell University Press, 2003.

Rubenstein, Murray A., ed. *Taiwan: A New History*. New York: M. E. Sharpe, 1999.

Storey, Robert. *Taiwan: Old World Meets New Economy*. Melbourne and Oakland, CA: Lonely Planet Publications, 2001.

Taiwan: China Regional Maps. 2002–2003. Singapore, Periplus Travel Maps.

Index

Index

Index

Picture Credits

About the Contributors

CHRISTOPHER L. "KIT" SALTER spent three years teaching English at a Chinese university in Taiwan and has traveled to East Asia eight different times over a period of 30 years. He is a geographer who wrote his dissertation on eastern Taiwan, but has taught about the larger world of East Asia for decades at the University of California at Los Angeles and the University of Missouri–Columbia. He has also been involved in geography education and he is the first recipient of the National Geographic Society's "Distinguished Geography Educator" Award. He has also received the George J. Miller Award for Distinguished Service from the National Council for Geographic Education. He now lives on a small farm in mid-Missouri with his wife, Cathy, who is also a writer.

CHARLES F. ("FRITZ") GRITZNER is Distinguished Professor of Geography at South Dakota University in Brookings. He is now in his fifth decade of college teaching and research. During his career, he has taught more than 60 different courses, spanning the fields of physical, cultural, and regional geography. In addition to his teaching, he enjoys writing, working with teachers, and sharing his love for geography with students. As consulting editor for the MODERN WORLD NATIONS series, he has a wonderful opportunity to combine each of these "hobbies." Fritz has served as both President and Executive Director of the National Council for Geographic Education and has received the Council's highest honor, the George J. Miller Award for Distinguished Service.